EXISTENTIALISM & SOCIOLOGY

Gila J. Hayim

With a New Introduction by the Author

EXISTENTIALISM & SOCIOLOGY

The Contribution of Jean-Paul Sartre

Transaction Publishers
New Brunswick (U.S.A.) and London (U.K.)

New material this edition copyright © 1996 by Transaction Publishers, New Brunswick, New Jersey 08903. Originally published in 1980 by The University of Massachusetts Press.

Grateful acknowledgment is made to the following for permission to reprint copyrighted material:
Alfred A. Knopf, for quotations from *Search for a Method*, by Jean-Paul Sartre, translated by Hazel E. Barnes. Copyright © 1968 by Alfred A. Knopf, Inc.
Philosophical Library, for quotations from *Being and Nothingness*, by Jean-Paul Sartre. Copyright © 1956 by Philosophical Library, Inc.
Oxford University Press, for quotations from *From Max Weber*, translated, edited, and with an introduction by H. H. Gerth and C. Wright Mills.
New Left Books, London, for quotations from *Critique of Dialectical Reason*, by Jean-Paul Sartre, translated by Alan Sheridan-Smith, edited by J. Ree, New Left Books, London, 1976.

Library of Congress Catalog Number: 95-19861
ISBN: 1-56000-840-7
Printed in the United States of America

Library of Congress Cataloging-in-Publication Data

Hayim, Gila J., date.
    [Existential sociology of Jean-Paul Sartre]
    Existentialism and sociology: the contribution of Jean-Paul Sartre / Gila J. Hayim; with a new introduction by the author.
        p.   cm.
    Originally published: The existential sociology of Jean-Paul Sartre. Amherst: University of Massachusetts Press, 1980.
    Includes bibliographical references and index.
    ISBN 1-56000-840-7 (paper: alk. paper)
    1. Sartre, Jean Paul, 1905-   . 2. Existentialism. 3. Sociology-Philosophy. I. Title.
B2430.S34H384   1995
194—dc20   95-19861
                                                                       CIP

To my mother

Contents

introduction to the

Transaction edition:

revisiting Sartre

The last decade has been a most turbulent period, both in terms of intellectual tension and global political upheaval. Both the concept of the individual-as-subject and of social groups-as-collectivities passed through remarkable and often painful transformations. The better part of the 1980s was consumed by a major shake-up of the Western canon and by a serious rethinking of the "meaning-structures" of *humanism, selfhood,* and *objectivity.* A good part of the change in these meaning-structures had to do with a shift of emphasis away from consciousness, as constructive of structures of coherence and purpose, to that of language. In the past, it was held that thought served to ground our access to self and reality. Presently, self and reality are considered to be artifacts of linguistic and cultural action. This shift of perspective transforms notions of selfhood and self-knowledge into matters of self-deception.

The more recent intellectual sources for this turn, and the debates it has spawned, may be found in postwar intellectual thought in France, which prompted an unprecedented wave of anti-Enlightenment sentiment. Concepts such as of *self-identity, self-determination, historical integration, resolution of alienation, progress,* and so on, so central to Western self-understanding, were thrown out as just so much sophistry. Such concepts were viewed as part of a dangerous metaphysics that had paved the way for collective violence, at one extreme, and increased social policing of the individual, on the other.

Schwab, in his insightful foreword to Frank Manfred's study on neostructuralism, goes so far as to point out that Foucault, Lacan and Derrida have provided "more than isolated variations on anti-rationalist themes. They have reformulated and reoriented the anti-rationalist project."[1] He finds this development as "surprising and unexpected" in as much as postwar France was beholden to Hegelian, Marxian, and Husserlian traditions, as well as to the specially French existential orientation of Jean-Paul Sartre, which was, of course, also influenced by these traditions.

These developments are far too complex, vast and transdisciplinary for me to attend to them in this essay. One specific reason for such an anti-Enlightenment (or anti-rationalist) onslaught is the intellectual and political disaffection with grandiose philosophies of liberation, and with the industrial human subject taken up as a cult of unrealistic historical possibilities. One may also consider the attack as a reaction to the radical emphasis on *consciousness* and its power for self-determination articulated, for example, by critical theorists and phenomenologists, but even more notably by the somehow heroic, conflict-tempered existentialism of Sartre. To be sure, Sartre was ever committed to defending the principle of self-determination, but without, however, wishing to merge the human subject into a cult. Sartre rejected prefigured visionary programs, essentialist views or fixed attribution of the human group, because humanity, in his view, is never a "completed project" but always a project in the making, one which continuously loses and reinvents itself in terms of social membership and in terms of natural systems in the physical world. Sartre says we should not believe "[t]hat there is a humankind to which we might set up a cult....The cult of humankind ends in the self-enclosed humanism of Comte, and let it be said, of fascism. This kind of humanism we can do without."[2] Sartre bound up his intellectual and practical life to the explication of the process of *self-determination* and the defense of *human freedom*. For Sartre, these are ultimate values, not merely theoretical and abstract notions, but aspects of a continuous personal and social struggle tied to concrete human needs and ends. The value of *freedom* reveals itself, Sartre insists, when it contends with its obstacles, that is, *freedom exhibits itself in the act of resistance*. It is through resistance to my given situation that my freedom is given meaning.

It is clear enough that Sartre was among the first to reject any notion of fixed self-identity, as well as agendas for an integrated, and unified human history. He was likewise suspicious of the classical dialectical systems of thought that speak of vague and imponderable universal *overcoming,* which was held to signify the complete resolution of social and material alienation by new forms of synthesis that occur in the symbolic and material reproduction of life. Sartre was among the first to make a break with the type of "closed humanism" that presupposes a unified and coherent human nature, fixed for all time, or a type of human nature that is alienated only by specific forms of social and political organization. Such a break with classical dialectical thought questions tenets of both bourgeois humanism bent to capture that which endures and remains stable (Husserl), as well as structural formalism aimed at predictions of historical evolutions and prefigured revolutions (Marx). With this break, Sartre may have, ironically, influenced and provided support to some new discourses in social-political and social-psychological theory, for example, in the poststructuralist and the feminist literature, especially in the latter's debate on 'essentialism' and on its implications for sexual identity.[3] In a highly readable and well-researched study by Howells, the author asserts such influence by Sartre, particularly on Derrida, even as the latter contested and rejected Sartrean humanism. Howells says:

> The decentered subject, the "death of man"...the rejection of Hegelian dialectics and the recognition of the impossibility of ultimate synthesis—such notions are more commonly associated with Lacan, Levi-Strauss, Foucault, Derrida and Lyotard than with Sartre, but a close reading of [Sartre's works] shows them to have been, at least in part, of Sartre's making.[4]

While Sartre may have been influential in prompting a reconsideration of the classical notion of the *historical subject,* it is clear that his comprehensive conception of the human subject, and his ethical outlook regarding individual and social rights and responsibilities, remain radically and fundamentally different from the positions of the poststructuralists and the deconstructionists. Sartre upholds, as they do not, a passionate commitment to human prerogative for self-determination and autonomy, coupled with an exacting ethos of responsibility that goes along with it.

To be sure, already in *Being and Nothingness,* Sartre prepared the way for a new concept of the subject and of "subjectivity," which challenged head-on the structuralist view, predominant in the sociology of his time, of a preconstituted individual, a view that was required for a static and stabilizing social theory, which Sartre rejected also. He also called into question the myth of progress as some "inevitable script" in history, a non-Sartrean notion notoriously consistent with a Hegelian-Marxist tradition of social theory. In Sartre's view, human subjectivity and human history are not fixed, they do not develop by an *a priori schemata,* but evolve through various and diverse forms of indefinite open-ended struggle, constantly tied to the dynamic freedom of others, with ever-changing group affiliations and social memberships, all in the midst of the crushing exigencies of "worked matter." Instead of the structuralist and functionalist view of the self, Sartre characterizes the self as an activity that is in "perpetual surpassing toward a coincidence with itself that is never given." It is this indefinite transformation of the individual and the social group toward a state which is not present and which is always ahead of the actor that constitutes the meaning of existential freedom, and let it be said, of its gnawing anguish and responsibility.

Continuity—Sartre's later works

When I completed my book on Sartre in 1980, which happens also to be the year of his death, there were very few studies that dealt with the first volume of his *Critique of Dialectical Reason.* I was not aware at the time of the existence of a single work in English, that dealt with both *Being and Nothingness,* his early major work, and the *Critique,* published twenty years later, and in relation to sociological concerns. In my book, I tried to show the thematic connections between the two works and how they may enrich social categories of analysis, particularly in relation to the themes of selfhood, the individual and the group, reciprocity and conflict, solidarity and deflection, and in the various forms of human affiliations and memberships. Rather than continuity, the dominant position prevailing then in the scholarship around Sartre claimed an intellectual discontinuity between the *Critique* and Sartre's early works, and a rift that quickly took on the term *radical conversion*. The controversy involved whether the shift to the position taken in the *Critique of Dialectical Reason* was a shift from the ontology of human freedom, found in *Being and Nothingness,* to a social condition based on recognized exigencies of materiality and necessity, derived largely from Marxism, which is found in Sartre's later work. I argued then, as I would now, that the phenomenology of individual consciousness in *Being and Nothingness* was indispensable and necessary for understanding the social categories in the *Critique of Dialectical Reason,* and that *Being and Nothingness* anticipated the thematic social concerns and ethics of the later work. The *Critique of Dialectical Reason* would never have come into being without the presupposition of human freedom and its presupposed manifestations and forms of externalization in society and in the material world of Nature. And rather than abandoning freedom in favor of necessity, Sartre established the social and historical vulnerability of freedom.

Sartre problematizes the idea of human freedom by situating it amidst the exigencies of materiality, in the world of institutional birth and decay, and in the world of human relationships and their costs. But in both works, I suggested, the concept of freedom, whether treated as an ontological *lack* (i.e., desire) as in *Being and Nothingness,* or as a social *need,* in the *Critique,* the concept posits common issues and stimulates social action. To be sure, the concept of necessity was not a new one in the *Critique,* I argued. Sartre already dealt with the notion of necessity in *Being and Nothingness,* where he explicates related concepts such as *en-soi,* the *Other,* and the *Situation.* Human intersubjectivity and self-situatedness in the world of materiality, Sartre says, operates at the most elementary level of existence, at the primary level of self-constitution and perception itself.

On the question of continuity in the work of J. P. Sartre, I was both curious and anxious awaiting Sartre's subsequent writings, published posthumously and after the completion of my own book. In Sartre's *Notebooks for an Ethics,* written about five years after *Being and Nothingness,* published in 1983 and translated into English in 1992, Sartre's commitment to human freedom continues, this time adding innumerable perspectives on the topic and a greater tendency to ground his thought in concrete illustrations, and in mundane situations of human social existence.[5] This volume, containing two books and two appendices, was approximately six hundred pages, to a large degree unorganized and unpolished, and is also the work that Sartre promised at the conclusion of *Being and Nothingness*. But the defense of human freedom and the struggle to promote it, remained for Sartre the organizing principle of his thinking. In the *Notebooks* he recaptures the notion of "transcendence," central to *Being and Nothingness*. He uses it to refer to the act of lifting up the self from the weight of the surrounding inertia, and also the daily act to re-establish and sometimes reinvent the common social bond. Just as in *Being and Nothingness,* the notion of "transcendence" in the *Notebooks* is drawn beyond the present toward the idea of possibility and freedom. The concept signifies the human capacity to stand back and identify world and self without permanently being this world and this self. McBride, in his extensive inquiry into Sartre's later works, says that throughout the entire evolution of Sartre's work, Sartre "never abandoned his bedrock conviction that free self-determination was both a human possibility and the only basis for a worthwhile human life."[6]

Despite the considerable lack of thematic order and conceptual guidance, Sartre's *Notebooks for an Ethics* is a rich resource book that deals with a great number of social and socio-psychological themes, which get presented in daily life, and which await their proper sociological unveiling. This is where Sartre begins the fledgling project of connecting the ontological with the social, which he will resume more systematically in the subsequent two volumes of the *Critique of Dialectical Reason,* more than a decade later. Toward that end he relentlessly rejected, as he did throughout his intellectual and political life, all forms of determinism that devalue the creative capacity of the individual as a member of a group, or the group as a collectivity of individuals, either to challenge, to recreate or to transcend its situation. In one section in the *Notebooks,* Sartre imaginatively qualifies the deterministic relationship that Marx, for example, posits between structures of consciousness, as they exhibit themselves in daily cultural activity, and their material and social situations. According to Sartre,

> The connections among the structures of the historical fact are much "looser" than Marx would have liked them to be. This is necessary since the individual is not a reflection but transcendence and invention. It is not false therefore that each of his works reflects his situation and expresses it. But this work expresses this situation by "surpassing it." And surpassing it is "not to negate it (antithesis) but to invent something on its basis."[7]

Sartre goes on to theoretically limit the conditioning force of habit and of repetition, and the leveling effect of the public ideas and structures of the "general" and the "average," which taint daily human life with inertia. In illustrating this point, he selects a most mundane activity, lifts it out of its everyday "general" framework or banality and imbues it with the singularity of invention. He writes about

> thousands and thousands of similar evenings in a restaurant next to the water. Each time, invented, reinvented, and parallel to all the rest. The *general* can be reinvented. As when in a family, every time the opportunity arises someone reinvents the word that expresses the family spirit. Never mechanical: the circumstances are never the same, one uses it in a slightly different manner, the humor is that one uses it here where no one in the family has ever used it before.[8]

Written roughly five years after *Being and Nothingness,* Sartre's *Notebooks* preserves the phenomenological temperament of the former work without, however, its excessive technical language and disciplined analysis. It opens up new angles and perspectives on earlier and new themes. We find, for example, new aspects and applications for the master/slave drama, a number of highly rich and original pieces on violence, on oppression, on acceptance, on refusal, on ignorance and failure, on prayer and demand, and then on love, on generosity and on the good—with a tentative attempt to find an impressionistic synthesis between aesthetical and ethical-social sensibilities, as illustrated, for example, in his treatment of the idea of the "good." What is perhaps significant in this work is the manner in which Sartre struggles to translate and connect his phenomenological categories into concrete situations anchored in social experience and historical reality. For example, Sartre anticipated the theme of the *practico-inert*, as the externalized fixation of our freedom in matter, a historical-phenomenological theme that later on dominates the *Critique*. There is the dramatic image of the material environment absorbing our labor, only to produce its own second-order consequences notwithstanding our intentions. This is an uncannily insightful forward look into what is now our present ecological predicament; here Sartre properly reflects upon the idea of the "engineer." The *practico-inert* partly signifies the unintended consequences of the original and free human design or choice, consequences that defy or turn against the original choice and become antihuman, as for example in the process of ecological decay, environmental pollution, and so on. Both in the *Notebooks,* and later on in the two volumes of the *Critique of Dialectical Reason,* our human choices and their unintentional effects and objects, remain bound to one another, and remind us of the early dialectics of the *pour-soi* and the *en-soi*. These concepts refer to a constant interplay between intended acts of objectification incurred by the actor, and their consequences that co-constitute, at least in part, the actor's objectivity.

In the relatively unpolished *Notebooks,* Sartre sets out tentatively, oftentimes in fragments and undeveloped headlines, to analyze categories of the *ethical* and the *social*. He speaks of the need to evaluate universal principles in light of the dynamics of the ever-changing social reality of the human group. He expresses this theme at the outset when he says: "To whom is the ethical demand addressed? To the abstract universal? But then it loses all its meaning and becomes abstract and formal itself, since the concrete, that is, social-situation may change. If one says, 'Act in such a way, other things being equal,' this demand loses all its meaning since it refers to the *eternal return*."[9] According to Sartre, universal principles of *ethics,* of *the good* and of *freedom* are meaningless, until anchored in the concrete world of individual and social situations and events. This simple questioning of the static Kantian ethics leads to a practical ethics of social engagement, which Sartre takes up in his inquiry into the idea of the *good*.

Toward the very end of the *Notebooks,* in an appendix titled "Good and Subjectivity," Sartre, writing while en route to the United States, says: "The good has to be done. This signifies that it is the end of an act, without a doubt. But also it does not exist apart from the act that does it."[10] Whatever *a priori* forms of good that can be said to exist in and by themselves are false idols or *nonsense,* Sartre continues, for the good needs to pass "through us." It is only the act itself that confers on the deed the attribute of the good, for it is not a term of knowledge.

Earlier in the *Notebooks,* Sartre refers to criticism against him, criticism that he speaks more of *refusal* and of *negation* of existence than of its *affirmation*. But *affirmation,* he responds, comes precisely from the ability to tear away from pre-existing and limiting determinations, in order to carve out a new reality from the full field of being, to condemn a given situation as oppressive and unbearable when judged in light of an alternative. Hence, doing the *good,* just like becoming "revolutionary," is an act of "uprooting from indifference," or, otherwise put, negating the inertia of the given situation through action: the *good* is itself an affirmative creation in relation to a prior negation; negation is the midwife of affirmation.[11] Transforming the ontological notion of the *good* as an individual act into socialized politics of resistance to ignorance, oppression and inertia, becomes the moment of redemption of the human group. Sartre calls this group the *group in fusion,* a theme that is continued and taken up systematically in volume 1 of the *Critique of Dialectical Reason.*

Roughly two-thirds of the way into the second volume of the *Critique,* written over a decade after the *Notebooks,* and published after his death, Sartre again merges historical-sociological categories with ontological concepts introduced much earlier in *Being and Nothingness*. He speaks about the relationship between the singularity of individual activ-

ity and the group, between *praxis* and *process,* objectification and objectivity, and other categories mediated by the
early concepts of the *in-itself* and the *for-itself,* discussed in
my book in reference to the first volume of the *Critique.*
Sartre's return to his early ontology when concluding the
second volume of the *Critique* has baffled even some of his
better interpreters. Aronson finds the shift to ontology *dis-
concerting* and asks: "Is he [Sartre] seeking to absorb *Being
and Nothingness* within the framework and terms of the
Critique?"[12] But of course, Sartre has been insinuating that
throughout the two volumes of the *Critique.*

Across the different points of Sartre's social thought, the
individual comes across as an active and constituting agent,
whose practice embodies the intending consciousness of an
actor, that is, as the *for-itself.* Totalized matter, the *in-itself,*
is the concretized world of materiality, which also reflects
back massified human actions. The individual, as a member
of the group, recognizes and defines the self partly through
worked or *totalized* matter (as in identifying with one's products, tools, institutions, computers and so on). In this connection Sartre defines *totalized matter* as...[the] vampire
object [which] constantly absorbs human action, lives on
blood taken from man and finally lives in symbiosis with
him."[13] The freedom of human practice and the lack of freedom of *seriality* or the *practico-inert* are always interlocked.
The unintended consequences of the original free choice
come back as anti-human, non-human, or quasi-human objectivity, affecting the life of the group as well as the acting
subject. Each human realization "entails modifications from
afar, of other objects and men within the practical field, the
action of each person is reconditioned by his own products"
concludes Sartre, years later.[14]

The exigencies of the "inert" largely signify the huge system of economic activity and its enormous enterprise of labor that guarantees human survival. In assuring our survival,
it does not mean, Sartre adds, that the process is an objective
one, or a fate in nature independent of human intervention.
Nor does it mean that it is completely benevolent, devoid of
exploitation and social catastrophies, or that it is concerned
with preserving the life of the working mass. The massive
material world around us (including its hardware and ma-

chines), which parades as an *objective* independent reality, is actually, to a large measure, also the sum consequence of our deeds and of our needs. What Sartre wants to emphasize is the original premise that constitutes the heart of his system, namely, that we cannot confer more reality on the world (*en-soi*) than on the human component in it (*pour-soi*) nor can we consider the human element as the simple product or output of the world system. The material-social world, in its entirety, is co-constituted by human needs. Sartre expresses the thought in his later writings in the following way: "[N]either the practico-inert, nor oppression, nor exploitation, nor *this* given alienation, would be possible if the huge, ponderous socio-economic machine were not sustained, conditioned, and set in motion by *needs*."[15] Human needs are infinite and never wholly fulfilled, which can be held to account for human social struggle and human history. The tendency to consider human needs as a determining objective structure that may refute the possibility of human freedom is too constrained and artificial, in my view. For Sartre, needs are not only physical or related to nature, but also constitute the *lack* that impels us toward each other in the co-constitution of our social, ethical and political life and values.

I find untenable the criticism that collapses the theoretical connection between *Being and Nothingness* and Sartre's later works, including the second volume of his *Critique,* to the simple duality of some *interior* and *exterior* worlds, or that of an *abstract freedom* supposedly distinguishing *Being and Nothingness* in contrast to a *practical freedom* in the *Critique*.[16] Such reading of Sartre, which completely polarizes his system of thought, simply does not follow from his work. Sartre's existential and social analysis is premised on the essential idea that consciousness and world are co-constituted. The person, Sartre consistently believed, is both *transcendence* and *facticity,* both subject and object, both self and other. Sartre reminds us of this social-psychological position in the *Critique* when he says: "It is impossible to *exist amongst men* without...my subjectivity getting its objective reality through them."[17] Interconnection with the material world, and intersubjectivity in the human world, exist at every level of self-constitution. Sartre might add that it is only in the ethics of bad faith that we cancel or nullify or obviate one or another of the dimensions of being.

A somewhat different view of Sartre's completed work across several decades is articulated by McBride. McBride speaks of his dismay (which I, incidentally, share) that Sartre's posthumously published work upset McBride's argument: "that there was greater continuity than discontinuity in Sartre's thought as a whole." As McBride wrote in 1987: "[T]hroughout all the new or newly discovered twists and turns, it is clear, at least to me, that Sartre's thinking about morals retained considerable fundamental continuities, and that I had already grasped some of its abiding themes almost a quarter century ago."[18]

The singularity of events against the universality of ideas

A crucial aim in Sartre's later works is to reconsider and largely reject the classical dialectic of social conflict and its utopian resolution. In both the *Notebooks* and in the second volume of the *Critique of Dialectical Reason*, Sartre de-emphasized the rhetorical utopian finality of Hegel and Marx, which utopian view is heavily geared toward universal integration and historical synthesis. If anything, the dialectic of social life, in Sartre's view, is guided by reinventions and inversions of past practice rather than by progressive integrations. Every great discovery differentiates the preceding epoch, as it were. Historical structures are indeterminate and may carry both destructive or constructive possibilities. Sartre saw the universalizing and unifying themes in social theory as conceptually different from the living action of the concrete social group. The idea of the *universal*, Sartre writes, "let fall outside of History the *history* lived by men from day to day."[19]

In the *Notebooks*, Sartre already spoke about some of the massive disenchantments and disappointments that we experience today in relation to the grand theoretical vistas of *class struggle*, the *unity in diversity*, the *dialectical progress of Reason*, and so on. Metaphysical goals, presented in a spirit of total inevitability and utmost seriousness, distort the meaning of action and oppress human life options and ways of understanding the world, while conferring more reality on abstract structures in the future than on the human component in it. Twenty years after writing the *Notebooks* Sartre remained skeptical about *universalizing discourses*. In an interview with an Italian journal, given in August 1969 and published under the title *France: Masses, Spontaneity, Party,* Sartre himself located revolutionary consciousness not in the class or in the party, *but in the transformative process of struggle itself.* Consciousness is born in actual struggle and "the class struggle only exists insofar as there exist places where an actual struggle is going on....In order that there should be consciousness and struggle, it is necessary that somebody should be fighting."[20]

Throughout his work, Sartre's suspicion of orthodox Marxism is painful and unrelenting. This guided my reading of both his early and later work, despite the large number of scholarly reviews of Sartre's work that stubbornly stick to the famous *conversion* hypothesis. During a conflict-laden phase in his intellectual development, in which he made an intentional endeavor to come to terms with Marxism, Sartre continued to attack what he referred to as the *violation of experience* by orthodox doctrines. In Sartre's *Search for a Method,* a treatise that contains the closest links to Marxist thought, Sartre asks: "Why has existentialism preserved its autonomy? Why has it not simply dissolved into Marxism?"[21] He responds by identifying the tension between the theoretical construction of *historical materialism,* as an *a priori* doctrine of the universal, and that of the concrete factual reality found in common human practice and social existence. In Sartre's view, orthodox Marxism never resolved the tension but instead separates theory from reality by making theory into fixed and timeless knowledge, and by transforming practice into *empiricism without principles.*

A decade after the publication of *Search for a Method,* in a chapter titled "The Social History of the Soviet Union," which appears in volume 2 of the *Critique of Dialectical Reason,* published after Sartre's death, he again discusses Marxist dogmatism and offers an original and serious analysis concerning the deformation of human practice. He gives us a historical analysis of the social history of the bureaucratic leadership of the Soviet Union and describes immobilization of human *praxis* into *nonpraxis,* its opposite, which Sartre refers to as *hexis.* The inertia and impotence of the masses coincides with the petrifying effects of the gigantic enterprise of industrialization, and with its bureaucratic rigidity. Here, Sartre chooses to use the concept of *totalization,* referring to all the integrative and complex technical processes of the socialist project, which defy analysis in abstract universalistic categories. Sartre alerts us to the importance of paying attention to dimensions of temporality, of locality and of concrete events, that traversed and reflected again and again in this massive effort to build the Soviet nation; the most gigantic enterprise in the history of the species, to which Sartre devoted almost half of the second volume of the *Critique.*

Totalization of knowledge, violation of experience, analysis that becomes *simple ceremony,* are strong terms that "criss-cross" Sartre's work. Sartre's consistent and relentless use of such critical terminology and his attack of doctrines that carry dogmatic presuppositions and fixed foundational principles clearly anticipate and correspond to the disaffection we see today with theoretical positions that over-assimilate, and gloss over differences and particularities. Universalistic doctrines, writes Sartre, which inflexibly refuse to differentiate among constituents, promote acts of suppression.[22] Sartre's conviction that one cannot replace a particular event by a universal idea prompted him to oppose both organistic and utopian inclinations in social theory, abstractly posited as the so-called *end of history,* or in ideas such as the *perfect community,* the *universal subject,* and so on. A human life, an event in culture, a particular human act, and so forth, cannot be transformed into generalized universals without dissolving life and culture in *a bath of sulphuric acid.* But Sartre, I think, should be corrected here, for it seems that all of the nineteenth century and the better half of the twentieth are best characterized by the universal and unifying impact of industrialization, and with it a particular relationship of labor to nature. Our disaffection today with generalized and all-inclusive worldviews may stem partly from downsizing the massive machine and the transvaluation of the political, ideological and social value of physical labor, in light of the advent of the softer infrastructure in the age of information.

To reiterate the theme of *continuity* in Sartre's thought, let it be said that much of the position just analyzed was anticipated in his "Materialism and Revolution," written twenty years before the *Critique*. The article contains a serious and patient elaboration of Sartre's disquiet with those who identified the generalized notion of *materialism* with a revolutionary state of being and acting. This was an identification fashionable in the 1940s, and may still be stylish today. One can affirm the crushing oppression and nonfreedom of the structures of the material world and identify with the suffering of the oppressed before becoming a materialist.[23] For Sartre, materialism does not make one revolutionary, but rather it is the all too human struggle to face up again and again to the oppressive societal situation in which one is placed.

A person becomes a *revolutionary,* in the Sartrean sense, only as the person ties social understanding to commitment to engage in social action, to the very point of risking one's life. Nor is *inner freedom* at odds with the *material position*. Indeed, both are a stoical hoax, a nonrevolutionary and empty intention on the part of the oppressed. The *inner freedom* of the *slave* is of no concrete consequence to the oppression of the *master*. In addition, the mere doctrine of *materialism* in fact plays into the hands of the master. It is the master who emphasizes the material *thing-hood* and *objectness* of the slave, which the latter internalizes as his own sphere of self-constitution, self-image and social objectivity: "Since the slave is a pure object [for the master] his education internalizes this objectivity."[24]

Ideology and terror: human practice and its inversion

Sartre deals with the spiral of defeat and reorganization in the history of the socialist dream, not as isolated manifestations or chronological ones, but as a series of cycling and returning events, interspersed by temporal possibilities whose future actuality cannot be prefigured. This contextual, dynamic, time-sensitive method of understanding a social history, Sartre intended to develop as the method of *critical dialectics,* as a constructive abandonment and reaction to what he saw as Marxist methodological limitations, which he highlighted in *Search for a Method*. The real meaning of

the dialectic has been obscured by *orthodox Marxism,* says
Sartre, by subordinating particular acts in human experience,
to preconstituted and general categories. The preconstituted
categories treat social historical events of the present as frozen entities, isolated from the life and death drama of human
practice. It is Sartre's recognition of the interventive power
and historical role of such concrete mediations as the family,
the particular historical act, the specific group relation, the
historical singularity of the leader, and so forth, that must
have impelled him to devote a substantial portion of his analysis and thinking in the second volume of the *Critique* to the
phenomenon of Stalin and Stalinism. In this work, Sartre reminds the reader of the *enveloping totalization* of specific
historical givens and historical individuals, Stalin being one
of those *specificities* who embodied enveloping social-his-
torical circumstances, circumstances that he himself co-cre-
ated, or co-orchestrated, just as circumstances created him.
Stalin is analyzed neither as bloodless abstraction, nor as a
metaphor for a dictatorial process of worldwide consequence.
In fact, one might even sense that awe fills the pages in which
Sartre first approaches the question of Stalin in the context
of the massive project of a failing socialism. Stalin is the result not only of social transformations, but also of a specific
personality and *person.* The terror of Stalin is also the fact
that "terror chose itself through Stalin."[25] That is, the common practice required *incarnation* in the form of an
individual's real action. But it is still this specific Stalin, a "patient militant, slow-witted, tenacious [individual] seeking to
discover the Russian truth progressively."[26] These characteristics led to Stalin becoming the material manifestation or
incarnation of the common social attitude, while at the same
time being the historical Stalin, or the singular chosen.

A lasting and most profound feeling remains after reading
this portion of Sartre's analysis. Sartre tries to depict one of
the most torturous and expansive undertakings in modern
history, One cannot help but be awestruck by the magna-
nimity of the vast human struggle for sustenance and historical and social meaning when, amidst scarcity and infinite violence, it hopes for a better future, as it tirelessly invents and
then inverts its world. The supreme realization is that human struggle remains magnanimous, at this scale of trouble,

even when it deviates, when it contravenes its own freedom, when it inverts its hour of opportunity, and then when it tumbles down and fails.

In "The Itinerary of a Thought," an interview that was given to *Left Review* in 1969, Sartre talked about his plans for volume 2 of the *Critique*. There, Sartre says, "I planned to develop a study of the objects constituted by entire collectivities with their own interests. In particular, I want to analyze the example of Stalin to see how the objects that constituted Stalinist institutions were created through the ensemble of relationships between groups and within groups in Soviet society, and through the relationships of all these to Stalin and of Stalin to them."[27] "The Itinerary of a Thought" also reflects the path that dominates volume 1 of the *Critique*. The two volumes, in fact, clearly intended to deal with the complex reflexivity and circular movement and interrelatedness of the individual as the member of the group, and of society as groups of individuals, and the forces of the material environment. Sartre emphasizes the singularity of the human factor in this system of relatedness enmeshed in the social processes and situations where common practice gets inverted, even as these situations, in part at least, generate from this same practice. Sartre concludes that the human factor is not a passive wheel in the total structure and system of society and history, but makes itself, for better or for worse, and remains the only accountable element in the process of social construction. Were it not so, the intelligibility of social action and of history itself would vanish at once, along with human responsibility. The question "What is history?" should always be turned into the relevant question "What is our history?" This is Sartre's major point in the 1969 "Itinerary" interview.[28]

In my own book, I alluded some years ago to Sartre's concern with intelligibility and the significance it has for the sociological enterprise. This attitude is especially noteworthy at a time such as ours. Our present mood is characterized by the rejection of human consciousness, its critical and revolutionary powers, its capacity to generate ideals and normative footholds beyond an ongoing daily basis for meaning, and by the rampant disaffection with the larger project of society and history as factors in liberation. Such a liberation project had been at the center of the Enlightenment thinking since long before its convenient sociological association with either Hegel or Marx. Both on the level of academic social analysis, and on the level of everyday activity, we experience fewer stable points of reference, greater complexity due to increased contingencies in social life, and increasingly less control over social and personal outcomes and results. It is probably at times such as these that Sartre's thoughts about the individual, society and history regain relevance. Sartre warns against the *spirit of seriousness,* which falsely gives a narrow technical status to the given material realities and institutional apparatus of social change. Such a *spirit of seriousness* confers more reality to the world than to the human element in it, and approaches the constituted world as absolute and independent of human volition. Such spirit engenders ethics of an individual's helplessness, and a passive adaptation to the iniquities of social life. It cancels out intelligibility that is crucial to Sartre's method, namely, that behind the façade of orders of societies and continuities in history, lies a real human value based in actual practice.

Sartre's social analysis interlocks large-scale historico-ethical events with the lived experience of social actors in the world of daily life. One gains an experientially based recognition in one's self and others, of the movement between moments of self-determination and inertia, between the exhilarating freedom in the intentional act and the often painful recognition of its unintended consequences. There is a constant relationship of social reciprocity between the human actor and the social fields and products of that actor. *There are local histories within history.*

The human group, in Sartre's view, is alone the foundation of the moral order of humanity. That this humanity is indeterminate and of no "fixed nature" should not commit us to mindless nihilism, but on the contrary, may lead us to recognize the profound implications of freedom and the awesome responsibility attached to it. Meaningfulness of action lies in our socialized recognition of each other and of the earth. The *creation of values* remains, therefore, the supreme act in our intersubjective social constitution. An engaged existence impels us repeatedly and open-endedly to recognize each other as social beings involved in mutual *value mak-*

ing. To a significant degree, value building guides the spirit that fills Sartre's later work on social life and ethics. It is biographically relevant to note, also, that Sartre laboriously tried to complete his work in the face of progressive loss of sight.

Throughout his work, Sartre transforms individual experience and social life into an existence engaged in integrating moments of passion and ethics. The moment of passion comes through the act of choice and the power to commit the self in this act. The ethical moment is no less active, and signifies the nullification of bland indifference. Sartre concludes: "[E]thics is the theory of action. But action is abstract if it is not work and struggle."[29] This is not *blind* action. It is action guided by the soulful realization that the possibilities that one *is* belong also to another.

Gila J. Hayim
Brandeis University
Waltham, Massachusetts
1995

Notes

I thank Dr. Irving Louis Horowitz for his input and critical reading of my essay and Mr. David Allen for his continued interest in my work and valuable editorial notes to this new introduction.

1. Manfred Frank, *What is Neostructuralism?*, trans. Sabine Wilke and Richard Gray; foreword by Martin Schwab (Minneapolis: University of Minnesota Press, 1994), p. xiii.
2. Jean-Paul Sartre, *Existentialism and Human Emotions* (New York: The Wisdom Library, 1957), p. 50.
3. See for example, Chris Weedon: *Feminist Practice and Poststructuralist Theory* (New York: Basil Blackwell, 1987).
4. Christina Howells, *Sartre: The Necessity of Freedom* (Cambridge University Press, 1988), p. 194.
5. Jean-Paul Sartre, *Notebooks for an Ethics*, trans. David Pellauer (Chicago: The University of Chicago Press, 1992).
6. William L. McBride, *Sartre's Political Theory* (Bloomington: Indiana University Press, 1991), p. 9.
7. Sartre, *Notebooks*, pp. 74-5.
8. Ibid., p. 75.

9. Ibid., p. 7.
10. Ibid., p. 555.
11. Ibid., p. 147.
12. Ronald Aronson, *Sartre's Second Critique* (Chicago: The University of Chicago Press, 1987), p. 185.
13. Jean-Paul Sartre, *Critique of Dialectical Reason,* vol. 1, trans. Alan Sheridan-Smith, ed. Jonathan Ree (London: NLB, 1976), p. 169.
14. Jean-Paul Sartre, *Critique of Dialectical Reason,* vol. 2, trans. Quintin Hoare, ed. Arlette Elkaïm-Sartre (London: Verso, 1991), p. 387.
15. Ibid., p. 388.
16. David Detmer, *Freedom as a Value: A Critique of the Ethical Theory of Jean-Paul Sartre* (La Salle, Ill.: Open Court, 1986), p. 129.
17. Sartre, *Critique,* vol. 1, p. 105.
18. William M. McBride, "The Evolution of Sartre's Conception of Morals," *Phenomenological Inquiry* (October 1987): p. 25.
19. Sartre, *Notebooks,* p. 80.
20. Jean-Paul Sartre, *Between Existentialism and Marxism,* trans. John Mathews (New York: Pantheon Books, 1974), p. 123.
21. Jean-Paul Sartre, *Search for a Method* (New York: Vintage Books, 1963), p. 21.
22. Ibid., p. 148.
23. Jean-Paul Sartre, *Literary and Philosophical Essays,* trans. Annette Michelson (New York: Collier Books, 1962), p. 215.
24. Sartre, *Notebooks,* p. 405.
25. Sartre, *Critique,* vol. 2, p. 213.
26. Ibid., p. 212.
27. Jean-Paul Sartre, "The Itinerary of a Thought," in Sartre's *Between Existentialism and Marxism,* p. 56.
28. Ibid., p. 54.
29. Sartre, *Notebooks,* p. 17.

acknowledgment

I am indebted to Professor Kurt H. Wolff for his generous assistance in reading, criticizing and editing portions of this book. I am equally grateful to Mr. David Allen for his unfailing help in editing the work and for his valuable comments.

To Mrs. Marilyn Aaron and Mrs. Gwen Whateley in the Sociology Department at Brandeis University who have assisted in many ways, I offer my thanks.

My special gratitude goes to Professor Marcia G. Weskott for our many stimulating talks on the subject matter of this work and all else.

My love goes to Rebecca, David, Benjamin, Haskel, Nava, Jacob and their families for being who they are and for the care and the ideal conditions they extended to me during my stay at U.C.L.A. in 1978 that made possible the writing of the larger part of this work.

Lastly, I thank Judge Ham N. Shumbi for the joy of debating with him and for his discerning reason, which have influenced this book and much else.

Gila J. Hayim

introduction

The controversy surrounding Sartre's social thought might have resulted from the novelty of his style, from the intimate manner in which he describes phenomena, and most importantly, from the fact that he chose humanity as his object of inquiry. We have become overly accustomed to technical analysis, a style of analysis which favors the description of the world of things over that of human actors. Technical reason inspires our faith since it continuously discovers unity and predictability in "worked matter," while in humanity it finds only fragmentation. We come to know ourselves in terms of the worked world of matter and the position we occupy in it. As an ensemble of materiality and organizations the world transcends us, and when we attempt to comprehend it, we comprehend it as the compelling object of our daily desires. Sartre identified the priority of the world of worked matter over human life as the "spirit of seriousness," or the "dismissal of human reality in favor of the world."

He found this hierarchy of values—world over humanity— to be perplexing, and he set out to re-evaluate it. In doing so he worked within a number of disciplines, including philosophy, sociology and psychology—disciplines which have established, in the last century, a variety of conflicting and problematic views of the human being.

Sartre laid down his method of social inquiry in two major works: *Being and Nothingness* and *Critique of Dialectical Rea-*

son. These works also served as a foundation for his particular
type of existentialism. But the existential motif in them is not
restricted to the prospect of salvaging human subjectivity in the
context of a *made world.* It is also used as a vehicle for breaking new ground in the study of social life. Moreover, the
existential motif of Sartre is not a limitation of perspective.
Contrary to what is conventionally believed, Sartre does not
concentrate on irrational aspects of human life, nor does he
deal solely with subjective dimensions of human reality. Such
a view is often developed within the context of a cursory and
incomplete analysis of his social writings. There is little affinity
between my work in this book and what appears in the literature as a "sociology of feelings," allegedly constituting the main
thrust of existential sociology.[1] There is sparse evidence in the
two major works of Sartre to any such claims.

For Sartre, a theory of existence *is* simultaneously a theory
of action. In the *Critique* in particular, Sartre develops a theory
of *social action* in which the individual actor, his social group,
and the field of his practical action are interconnected.

Being and Nothingness was published in 1943 and was received by scholars and laypersons alike as a radical statement
concerning human freedom. Its large size and difficult language
discouraged thorough examinations. It was criticized as a doctrine of despair and disenchantment,[2] as a revolt against intel-
lectualism and the world of ideas, and, by the layperson, as a
work of atheism.[3] In America it was even fantastically considered by some to be a work of pornography.[4] But more serious
analysis, especially in Europe, began to produce more favorable

[1] Jack D. Douglas, "Existential Sociology," in *Existential Sociology,*
ed. Jack D. Douglas and John M. Johnson (Cambridge: Cambridge
University Press, 1977), p. 3–73.

[2] Marjorie Grene, *Dreadful Freedom: A Critique of Existentialism*
(Chicago: University of Chicago Press, 1948), chapters three and four.

[3] Walter Kaufman, *Existentialism from Dostoevesky to Sartre,* ed.
with an introduction, prefaces and new translation (New York: New
American Library, 1956).

[4] *Ibid.* See p. 46 for Kaufman's discussion of this.

reviews and interpretations.[5] In Britain, the work of E. L. Allen
was among those early efforts in the English-speaking countries
to win for Sartre, and for existentialism in general, a wider and
an essentially academic recognition. In concluding his study on
Being and Nothingness Allen writes: ". . . I have been concerned to give as fair a presentation of Sartre's philosophy as
possible, and in particular to defend it against certain misun-
derstandings. I hope I have shown that it is not to be charged
with nihilism or solipsism, but is a real effort to afford moral
guidance for an age in which values are threatened and men
have lost the traditional authorities that once directed their
lives." [6]

Increased recognition gave rise to a number of excellent ex-
positions, summaries and commentaries, for example, by Desan,[7] Grimsley,[8] Catalano,[9] Stern[10] and Thody.[11] However, the
focus of these studies remained essentially philosophical or literary. Only Craib,[12] in a recent book, shows the beginning of
an effort to deal with social themes and concerns in Sartre's
work.

The Critique of Dialectical Reason was published approximately twenty years after *Being and Nothingness.* It was published along with a small essay entitled *Search for a Method*

---

[5] Francis Jeanson, *Le Probleme Moral et La Pensés De Sartre,* Lettre-
préface de Jean-Paul Sartre (Paris: Editions Du Myrte, 1947).

[6] E. L. Allen, *Existentialism from Within* (1953; reprint ed., West-
port, Conn.: Greenwood Press, 1973) p. 89.

[7] Wilfrid Desan, *The Tragic Finale: An Essay on the Philosophy of
Jean-Paul Sartre* (New York: Harper Torchbooks, 1960).

[8] Ronald Grimsley, *Existential Thought* (Cardiff: University of Wales
Press, 1967).

[9] Joseph S. Catalano, *A Commentary on Jean-Paul Sartre's Being and
Nothingness* (New York: Harper and Row, 1974).

[10] Alfred Stern, *Sartre: His Philosophy and Psychoanalysis* (New
York: The Liberal Arts Press, 1953).

[11] Philip Thody, *Jean-Paul Sartre: A Literary and Political Study*
(London: Hamish Hamilton, 1960).

[12] Ian Craib, *Existentialism and Sociology: A Study of Jean-Paul
Sartre* (Cambridge: Cambridge University Press, 1976).

which Sartre originally intended to append to the *Critique*.
Strangely enough, the smaller essay became the more popular
of the two works. This could be because it was translated into
English before the *Critique* and also because of its size. However, this is unfortunate, since *Search for a Method* is a political statement, originally written by Sartre as a contribution to
a Polish review. It was later altered and reprinted in *Les Temps
Modernes* under the title of "Existentialism and Marxism."
Search for a Method remains, essentially, a critique of the contradictions found in contemporary Marxist philosophy and practice, which Sartre condemns as being "orthodox," "simplistic,"
and "idealistic." One could say that in *Search for a Method*
Sartre attempted to correct shortcomings in Marxist methodology, a task which he followed up in the *Critique*. Aside from
that, the essay does not begin to touch upon the many themes
and concerns which constitute the *Critique*.

The publication of the *Critique* produced its own controversy.
This time the controversy centered around the issue of whether
there is continuity between *Being and Nothingness* and the
Critique. The question was whether or not the shift from the
concept of a radically free individual, in *Being and Nothingness,* to the somewhat socially and historically constituted individual, in the *Critique,* is not a betrayal of existentialism, as
well as a shift to a new doctrine. For example, the term "radical
conversion" appeared frequently in the literature. Sheridan's
book,[13] using the term in its title, summarizes the views of
some of these criticisms, notably those of Warnock.

A few expository books in English are available on the
Critique. One by Desan,[14] called *The Marxism of Jean-Paul
Sartre,* is an excellent, comprehensive work, and another, by
Raymond Aron, analyzes the political implications of the work.[15]

[13] James F. Sheridan, Jr., *Sartre: The Radical Conversion* (Athens,
Ohio: Ohio University Press, 1969).

[14] Wilfrid Desan, *The Marxism of Jean-Paul Sartre* (Gloucester,
Mass.: Peter Smith, 1974).

[15] Raymond Aron, *History and the Dialectic of Violence: An Analysis of Sartre's Critique de la Raison Dialectique,* trans. Barry Cooper
(New York: Harper and Row, 1975).

A third book by Craib, of lesser scope, deserves mention as well. I am not aware of a single work which treats *Being and Nothingness* and the *Critique* simultaneously and in relation to sociological perspectives and interest. My work is a modest attempt to do just that. I wish to identify the connection between *Being and Nothingness* and the *Critique* in Sartre's social thought. I also hope to establish the relevance of these two major works for sociology and for the social sciences in general, with respect to both method and content.

In emphasizing the sociological significance of these two works of Sartre, I do not deal with the history or method of philosophy, such as the relationship between Sartre and Descartes, Husserl or Heidegger. I have, however, dealt with the influence which Marx and Hegel had on Sartre's ideas. The section on the master-slave relationship in Hegel's *Phenomenology of the Mind* is particularly instructive when attempting to understand Sartre's concepts on the Self and the Other. By dealing with this aspect of Hegel's work I also hoped to make the sociological relevance of Hegel himself more known to the reader.

In *Being and Nothingness* Sartre speaks of the relation between human consciousness, essentially a structure of choice and action (*pour-soi*), and the social world (*en-soi*). The acting subject, or human consciousness, defined by Sartre as a "lack" or desire, is always in search of stability and permanency in the world. But since human action is future-oriented, it is directed toward a state of being which is not present, that is, toward possibility. The reaching out toward possibility is a distinctive feature of human freedom. However, human freedom can be a source of anguish, since freedom for Sartre entails responsibility. What the individual does with freedom and the responsibility which it exacts is the subject of Sartre's well-known concept of "bad faith." While here described only in rudimentary fashion, these concepts prepared the ground for Sartre's work on the *Critique* and facilitated Sartre's penetrating account of the life and fate of the human group. The earlier work on *Being and Nothingness* is brought up to its logical conclusion in the *Critique,* that is, the meaning and consequences of human freedom in the context of a socio-historical world. The world, for Sartre, is the *pragmata*, a world of objects which awaits human goals and human action (praxis) upon it.

In the last section of *Being and Nothingness* Sartre prefigures the thematic concerns which appear later in the *Critique*. He finds the modern individual increasingly ruled by the structures of the world outside him, with all the attendant consequences of such dependency: loss of courage and vision, and the spectre of spiritual annihilation. This is an account of the modern social group cluttered up with a world of quantity, averages, and mass-artifacts, which is of the group's own making and choice, but which has now turned against it with numerous consequences.

In chapter one I cover the basic concepts developed in *Being and Nothingness,* notably those of "temporality," "negation," "anguish" and "bad faith." These concepts are analyzed in conjunction with a number of sociological perspectives, such as Weber's notions concerning time, action and ethics.

My approach to Weber's social thought and to Sartre's work is at odds with some of the current literature. For example, in a review article on existential sociology, Peter Manning said: "Weber has established the centrality of man's goal-directed rationality; sociological existentialism sought to establish a framework for understanding the non-rational aspects of human life, especially the situated nature of the emotions." [16] I find that such a statement does not follow from either *Being and Nothingness* or the *Critique*.

In chapter two I move from the individual as the center of free action, to the individual in relation to the Other. For Sartre, the Other serves as an essential reference for the meaning of one's action and freedom. Types of interpersonal relations ranging from love and pledge relations to those of indifference and destruction are included. Far from being literary presentations of intimate types of human interaction, these relations reappear

[16] Peter K. Manning, "Existential Sociology," in *Contemporary Sociological Theories,* ed. Allen Wells (Santa Monica, Calif.: Goodyear Publishing Co., 1978), p. 335.

in the *Critique* to define concrete collective behavior of social groups, notably that of the praxis group and the serial group, which are analyzed in chapter five. The works of G. H. Mead and G. W. F. Hegel, on the Self and the Other, are also treated.

In chapter three I attempt to unify the perspectives in the first two chapters and present a theory of action. Three existential attitudes, namely *being, acting* and *possessing,* are integrated in the theory. The chapter also clarifies what Sartre calls "existential psychoanalysis."

In chapter four I introduce the reader to the *Critique* and establish its thematic links with *Being and Nothingness.* The earlier concepts of the *pour-soi* and *en-soi* are further developed in the *Critique.* They serve as a conceptual background against which Sartre portrays the struggle of the human group, the struggle for self-affirmation, and the overcoming of social inertia.

Sartre wishes to study the formation of social groups as these groups are produced by concrete individuals. He wishes to find out whether the emergence of human groups, their visions, conflicts, contradictions, and relations to matter and to each other, are intelligible. He sees that through contact with the material world—the practical field of daily existence—human beings "interiorize" the world, in that they discover themselves as objectivities in the world. Men see themselves as "products," "processes," "collectives," and so on. On the other hand men exteriorize themselves in that they act upon the world, thereby discovering that they are active agents. By exteriorizing themselves, they find themselves mediating different aspects of materiality. They even establish relations of matter to matter itself. The worked object gains in importance, in power and in meaning, to such an extent that it, in turn, begins to mediate the relationships among human beings themselves. The material world absorbs human praxis, and matter worked by labor constitutes a new identity for humanity. The worked object becomes the center of human communication and intersubjectivity. This is the concept of the practico-inert which reappears again and again in the *Critique.*

In this chapter I also deal with Sartre's concepts of totalization and necessity, concepts which constitute the existential critique of positive reason.

In chapter five, I analyze the ramifications of the concept of the practico-inert, which, for Sartre, is inseparable from human sociality. Two orders of human sociality appear: the serial group, which refers to the sociology of human inertia, and the praxis group, which is essentially a study in human revolt. I conclude my study of the praxis group with reference to the ideas of "fraternity" and its consequences of pledge and violence. Sartre's analysis of the transformation from one type of group to another offers one of the most compassionate accounts of social life and its fate.

In chapter six I deal with the concept of organization, which refers to the contradictions within the social group as it moves into advanced stages of social integration. A distinction is made between the analytical rationality of *process* and the simple concrete *praxis* of the individual. This raises one of the major and long-standing questions of sociology and refers to the problematics of collective ethics *versus* individual freedom. The opposition and identity of the individual and the group, of praxis and process, defines the essential theme of this chapter.

In chapter seven I cover the concepts of power and authority. The existential approach denies authority any foundation other than concrete human activity, thereby challenging the routinely adopted structural approach to the study of leadership, bureaucracy, complex institutions, governments and states. This chapter also amplifies Sartre's idea of common praxis which refers to the modern techniques of mass communication, mass control and education. Chapter eight deals with the idea of dialectical humanism and highlights essential concepts in the work by way of concluding it.

one

Freedom,

anguish and

bad faith

This chapter deals with basic concepts in *Being and Nothingness*. My analysis takes into account various sociological orientations, especially the work of Max Weber. Introducing Sartre in the context of sociological cognition should dispel any apprehension about Sartre's thought. The point which will be made is that Sartre does not primarily deal with "the absurd," "the obscure" or "the irrational" aspects of human life. One should of course pay attention to notions of the absurd or the irrational, since they are inescapable aspects of every reflective existence, but they are not the specific subject matter of *Being and Nothingness*. Sartre's goal is intelligibility, in that he wishes to study the relation between the abstract and the concrete. He reviews conventional themes concerning human nature, human action and human relations, and he re-evaluates these themes from the point of view of the concrete, acting individual. Sartre identifies existence as action; and existence, for Sartre, precedes those very theories which refer to it. Obscurity arises, in fact, when existence is interpreted from the point of view of theoretical consciousness or essence.

Weber's scholarly pursuits (for instance his studies of religion, modernity and bureaucracy) are not of specific concern to Sartre. Nevertheless, these two scholars share a genuine concern for the human enterprise in the world, and they take great pains in understanding it appropriately. Both take into account temporality as an important aspect of human action, and both are committed to studying the role of choice, values and goals in human life. What is common to both is the conviction that *voluntarism* is the basic principle of human action and social organization.

The fact that both Sartre and Weber share these orientations does not of course mean that Weber is an existentialist nor does it mean that Sartre is an interpretive sociologist. Instead of imposing such a conclusion, my task in this chapter is to extract the existential component of Weber's work, not as a professed philosophical position but as a tacit aspect of his sociology. At the same time I wish to analyze and elucidate Sartre's existentialism through the eyes of Max Weber.

I shall deal with five issues: (a) human action and time in Sartre and Weber, (b) time and freedom: the existential experience of absence, (c) freedom and anguish, (d) anguish and the spirit of seriousness and (e) voluntarism and the act of valuation. Before proceeding along these lines, however, I briefly discuss existence and existentialism. A more detailed exposition of Sartre's existentialism appears later in the chapter.

Existence

By refusing to separate thought from life Socrates probably represented one of the earliest forms of existentialism, that is, the philosophical view that knowledge and existence are inextricably bound together. The ancient Hebrew prophet offered another fascinating aspect of existentialism. Through the admonitions exchanged between him and his God, he called for the collapse of the abstract and the sacred into the mundane. While such images, drawn from early times, may provide an intuitive introduction to existentialism, they do not offer a precise, analytical formulation of the term. Still, instead of beginning this chapter with an analytical definition, I shall point to the manner in which Karl Jaspers deals with it. Existence, for Jaspers, is an index; it names properties without alluding to a certain content. Existence encompasses the empirical properties of being, either as matter or as the body, but it also stands for consciousness, in all of its acts of reality-constitution and intersubjective communication. Existence encompasses the labor of my thought and action as well as my total culture. But whether existence is used to refer to my empirical body, to my consciousness or to my culture, "in no case can it [existence] be grasped as though it were something in the world which appeared before us. Rather it is that in which all other things appear to us. In general, we do not appropriately cognize it as an object; rather we become aware of it as a limit." [1]

Jaspers deliberately avoids using analytical language which deals with cause and consequence, since in his view too much analytical clarity makes knowledge absolute and authoritarian. While such an attitude toward knowledge is sensitive, it cannot by itself offer a common structure for the term *existence* which can be agreed upon by other existential writers. Jaspers is influenced by both Kierkegaard and Nietzsche and has great admiration for and even a measure of intellectual identification with their types of existentialism. But Kierkegaard and Nietzsche, the two major progenitors of modern existentialism, differ from each other in substance and in temper. Though each questioned radically the confident rationality of the Western mind, Kierkegaard's existentialism emerged from a religious commitment to the idea of aloneness, while the existentialism of Nietzsche sprang forth from a need to see the end of religion. Neither do Kierkegaard's work and the work of many of the recent exponents of existentialism, such as Sartre, have much in common. Kierkegaard's work was motivated by his passion for subjectivity and by his belief that the human situation can never be completely externalized into action. For Sartre, the opposite is true. For him, a human being is the sum total of his acts; hence, there is no hidden essence or secret subjectivity. In the context of Sartre's work, existence is defined by and through one's acts. Existence cannot hide behind the pretext of inwardness or *potentia*. One is what one does.

Most philosophies dealing with human existence contain the theme of duality. We are familiar, for example, with the dis-

[1] Karl Jaspers, *Reason and Existenz,* trans. with an introduction by William Earle (New York: The Noonday Press, 1955), p. 54.

tinction between being and essence in Plato, with the mind-body duality of Descartes, the noumenon-phenomenon distinction in Kant, to mention only a few. These dualistic positions refer quite simply to the difference between "exterior" and "interior" worlds. Exterior reality is mere appearance, a false picture behind which stands true being, or potentia. Nothing which appears is its truth. Sartre attacks such a position. By his view each human act of expression indicates itself and conceals nothing. There is no difference between the external act and the inner potentia. The act exhausts all capabilities of the acting person who cannot make excuses by referring to the "hidden" capabilities of the self. In fact, description of the real is possible since the person manifests himself wholly. By Sartre's view one cannot speak of "genius" as a subjectively concealed fact, for the genius is that person who actually produces works of genius.[2]

Obviously there are an infinite number of modes in which personhood can be manifested. No thing can appear multi-sidedly and all at once. It can appear only in certain ways and it is constantly subject to change. What is revealed is merely *one* aspect of a plurality of aspects. A series of such revealed aspects of the thing gains synthetic unity by means of a variety of factors. Chief among these factors is, for example, the way in which we perceive an action in light of its aim. Sartre wishes to describe and comprehend human existence as it is manifested through meaningful sets of revealed aspects of the person.

Philosophers have long been puzzled by another duality, namely the separation of consciousness and the external world. Does consciousness (mind, knowledge, subjectivity) precede the world and its materiality or is it a product of the given world? An extreme position was taken by Berkeley, for example, who claimed that a table exists in the outside world because it is first perceived by a mind, that is, that the consciousness precedes the world. Sartre rejects this view and asserts that the independent existence of the world is a fact before conscious-

[2] Jean-Paul Sartre, *Being and Nothingness,* trans. Hazel E. Barnes (New York: Washington Square Press, 1973), pp. 4, 5.

ness. The existence of a table is not dependent upon one's consciousness of it. In fact, a table cannot exist in one's consciousness: it exists in relation to something other, to the right or left, near a window, and so on.[3] A table is not produced by knowledge, it is an object before my knowledge of it. Consciousness is consciousness of something other than itself. But consciousness is not ignorant of itself. It can be self-conscious, or reflective of the fact that it is aware of the table. More importantly, it can view itself as a mere object, as, for example, in the experience of shame or pride, moods which result from an act of passing judgment on ourselves as objects.

When speaking of the relation between consciousness and its object we speak of the relation between individual and world. Consciousness has no meaning by itself since it manifests itself as a desire for some object in the world. The world, in turn, has no intrinsic meaning since it has to be intended by human consciousness or human desire. Consciousness and object are co-constituted.

These statements may give the reader some idea of the diversity of approaches found in existentialism. A thematic unity could probably be deduced but only at the expense of oversimplification. Indeed, existentialists, with the exception of Sartre, are neither authors of technical philosophical systems, nor do they desire to be approached as such. I exclude Sartre from this general statement because in his works on social philosophy he makes a thorough attempt at synthesizing his existential insights and concepts into a system approaching what Fernando Molina refers to as "technical philosophical methodology."[4]

Human action and time in Sartre and Weber

Sartre attacks the natural scientific emphasis on objective structures as completely deterministic of human behavior. In the social sciences such emphasis has produced a methodology of society and history that is basically a methodology of inert ex-

---

[3] Ibid., p. 11.

[4] Fernando Molina, *Existentialism as Philosophy* (Englewood Cliffs, N.J.: Prentice-Hall, 1962).

teriority. It excludes a willed human life developing temporally into human history, and, in fact, human history becomes a special form of natural history. Sartre argues that immediate and lived praxis expresses itself actively in time. The person acts while relating himself to past, present and future, and thereby expresses social action reflectively. Moreover, the fact that a plurality of individual actions may become an institution does not justify neglect of the individual in favor of structural or institutional analysis. Structural analysis is important, but it cannot serve as the critical method which links action to time.[5] Atomization in analysis, in fact, occurs when we divide the living social reality into fixed and separate categories and structures. Such division is in step with *positivistic reason* whose end is intellection rather than comprehension.

Intellection is like explanation in the natural sciences—the explanation of the necessary and the inert as embodied in the world of things. "Things" have no intention or desire or temporality. On the other hand, comprehension, as the quality of the critical method, is the clarity one gains when one is involved in a project that is defined by its future goal. Comprehension results from an act *intended* by oneself or by another human being where there is consciousness of the ends sought. "Whenever a praxis [human action] can be traced to the intention of a practical organism or of a group . . . there is comprehension." [6]

In contrast, positivistic sociology emphasizes such concepts as "role," "structure," "external fact" and "process" as conditions relatively independent of the present desires and future goals of acting individuals. Human behavior is considered to be a function of such structural forces, regardless of individual ends or intentions. Human motivation, since it is "abstract," is considered too elusive and subjective a component of action to be necessary for understanding human behavior. This line of thinking can be found in most sociological investigations—from Durkheim to the present—which deal with the structural or

[5] Jean-Paul Sartre, *Critique of Dialectical Reason,* trans. Alan Sheridan-Smith, ed. Jonathan Ree (London: NLB, 1976), pp. 27, 56, 65.
[6] Ibid., p. 76.

institutional aspects of social reality. The explanatory power is assigned to the collective forces which constitute objective structures *vis-à-vis* human goals. Thus, positivistic sociology, as the allegedly scientific sociology, "is based on an assumption central to Durkheimian thought, the assumption that society is a reality different in kind from individual realities and that every social fact is the result of another social fact and never of a fact of individual psychology." [7] For Durkheim, it is the structure of the presently given society and its institutions which serves as the object of scientific analysis. Durkheim doubted that analysis of the past and the future is necessary for dealing with the phenomena sociology seeks to explain. Historical explanation, for him, is not true scientific explanation; less scientific still is any resort to the category of the future. This position is consistent with his idea that a social phenomenon is to be explained synchronically by means of the method of concomitant variation. Durkheim states that human needs and behavior are never voluntary or purposive but are the result of external determinations: "[T]he fact that we allow a place for human needs in sociological explanations does not mean that we even partially revert to teleology. These needs can influence social evolution only on condition that they themselves . . . can be explained solely by causes that are deterministic and not at all purposive." [8] Historical developments should not be explained as the realization of prior human intention or "of ends clearly or obscurely felt," but as the effects of social facts independent of human ends. If a social phenomenon happens to serve a human end, this is only incidental, and not the reason for the rise of that social phenomenon.

This line of thinking is alien to the existential mode of analysis, but it is also alien to the Weberian mode of analysis. Hu-

---

[7] Raymond Aron, *Main Currents in Sociological Thought, Vol. 2: Durkheim, Pareto, and Weber,* trans. Richard Howard and Helen Weaver (Garden City, N.Y.: 1970), pp. 77–78.

[8] Emile Durkheim, *The Rules of Sociological Method,* trans. Sarah A. Solovay and John H. Mueller, ed. George E. G. Catlin (New York: The Free Press, 1968), p. 93.

man experience for Weber, as for Sartre, is grounded in goals, goals which are diachronic. For this reason, the categories of past and future are cardinal points in Weber's analysis of any present social phenomenon. Historical and sociological types of analysis are methodologically and temporally related. The interdependence of history and society is the point of departure for Weber's major works. Interpretation of human orientation toward the future—an orientation which resides in one's attitudes toward goals—is indispensable for the adequate understanding of social action. This view is also the basis for his concept of *Weltanschauung* or "world view." The fact that human interests and actions can be governed by certain belief systems or world views is taken up in the thesis that is central to the famous work, *The Protestant Ethic and the Spirit of Capitalism.* Social organization can be influenced by interests that are future-oriented; these interests may be non-material and are often affected more by existential than by utilitarian factors. This does not mean that Weber ignored structural conditions external to the will and values of the individual actor. On the contrary, in "The Fundamental Concepts of Sociology" Weber made it quite clear that in the human sciences consideration should be given to "processes and phenomena which are devoid of subjective meaning." But he immediately qualifies this assertion by unequivocally demanding that at the same time the human component always be introduced into such analysis. For instance, while Weber mentions technology as an example of an external process "devoid of subjective meaning," he insists that "a machine can be understood only in terms of the meaning which its production and use have had or will have for human action. . . . Without reference to this meaning such an object remains wholly unintelligible. That which is intelligible or understandable about it is thus its relation to human action in the role either of means or of end; a relation of which the actor or actors can be said to have been aware and to which their actions have been oriented. Only in terms of such categories is it possible to 'understand' objects of this kind. On the other hand, processes or conditions, whether they are animate or inanimate, human or non-human, are in the present sense devoid of meaning in so far as they cannot be related to an intended purpose." [9]

Emphasizing human goals is a recurrent theme for Weber and, in fact, grounds his typology of action. For Sartre, too, the social world is defined by human goals; indeed, it is the fact that matter is worked upon by human desires and labor which gives us a world that is intelligible. For Sartre, as for Weber, the world harbors no meaning except that which has been created by human agents in accordance with their ends. Human action is not governed by the laws of nature, Sartre says (in contradistinction to Engels), for if it were, then the dialectical process of history would be unintelligible. In the social sciences, unintelligibility emerges precisely where I approach the forces of my environment as though they followed natural laws; that is, unintelligibility occurs when I reduce culture to nature.

For both Sartre and Weber, human ends constitute an irreducible order of things. As a matter of fact, these "irreducibles" mediate my comprehension of the non-human environment as well as of the actions of the Other. In Weber's words, "[W]e understand the chopping of wood or aiming of a gun in terms of *motive* in addition to direct *observation* if we know that the woodchopper is working for a wage or is chopping a supply of firewood for his own use. . . . Thus for a science which is concerned with the subjective meaning of action, explanation requires a grasp of the complex of meaning in which an actual course of understandable action thus interpreted belongs. In all such cases even where the processes are largely affectual, the subjective meaning of the action . . . will be called 'intended' meaning." [10] No doubt "intended" meaning rarely occurs in a pure context, but is mixed with affectual factors such as rage, anger and so on. The course of action can approximate the ideal type of meaningful action if it is recognized as taking place habitually within a typical complex of social conditions.

The possibility that human goals and ends are mere illusions

[9] Max Weber, "The Fundamental Concepts of Sociology," in *The Theory of Social and Economic Organization*, trans. A. M. Henderson and Talcott Parsons (New York: The Free Press, 1964), p. 93.

[10] Ibid., pp. 95–96.

is a permanent one, says Sartre, but the cancellation, or "stealing away," of human ends gives us the very notion of alienation and mystification,[11] or what he refers to as unintelligibility. Of special interest are examples which Sartre uses to illustrate this point. They are reminiscent of Weber's previous descriptions, used to explain the concept of *verstehen,* a concept which stands for "the interpretation of action in terms of its subjective meaning." [12] Sartre refers to the concept of *verstehen* without mentioning Weber; he defines it as the movement which confers meaning on the act as motivated by means of signification toward the future. "Man is, for himself and for others, a signifying being, since one can never understand the slightest of his gestures without going beyond the pure present and explaining it by the future. . . ." [13] For example, I can understand my companion's act when he suddenly starts toward the window as being motivated by the desire to let some air into an overheated room. In Sartre's words, "[i]n my companion's gesture, I see at once both his practical intention and the meaning of my discomfort. The movement of comprehension is simultaneously progressive (toward the objective result) and regressive (I go back toward the original condition)." [14] Nothing at all is inscribed on the structure of the environment itself; for instance, my companion's action is not inscribed in the temperature. It is *his* act which will now define the temperature as unbearable. Thus, structure gains its meaning from my directed activity, and it is this directed activity which creates for me a material situation, whether of obstacles or of possibilities. Human activity totalizes the environment—that is, it ascribes to it values which make it a means to an end—and in turn, the *totalized* environment defines human activity. This comprehension is nothing other than "the totalizing movement which gathers together my neighbor, myself, and the environment

[11] Jean-Paul Sartre, *Search for a Method,* trans. Hazel E. Barnes (New York: Vintage Books, 1968), p. 158.

[12] Weber, "The Fundamental Concepts of Sociology," pp. 94–95.

[13] Sartre, *Search for a Method,* p. 152.

[14] Ibid., pp. 153–54.

in the synthetic unity of an objectification in process." [15] For Weber, as for Sartre, comprehension amounts to the certainty a person gains when embarking on an action defined by its human goals.

Social structures, whether they appear as "stimuli," "results," "circumstances," "processes" or "conditions" (Weber), or as "tools," "instruments" or "material situations" (Sartre), should be defined in relation to a human undertaking. Sartre expresses this idea aptly when, in response to Durkheim's maxim to treat social facts as things, he says, "[S]ocial facts are things in so far as *all things* are, directly or indirectly, social facts." When social facts and conditions outside become meaningful, they are meaningful because inscribed on them are human properties, intentions, goals, possibilities or obstacles. It is these human properties, inscribed on the external conditions, that Sartre calls "significations." Significations come into being when a human event or value is carved into inanimate matter; they are a certain type of anthropomorphic representation which recognizes the human end in the material structure surrounding us. "[T]he relation to ends is a permanent structure of human enterprises and it is *on the basis of this relation* that real men evaluate actions, institutions or economic constructions." [16]

Human activity is grounded in absent or future objects. It cannot be understood without going beyond the present, given conditions. This human capacity for going beyond the present state of affairs toward "absence" is another distinctive feature of existential sociology.

The positing of a goal in the future is the positing of something that is absent, that is, not inscribed in the present circumstances. To realize the goal may mean to negate or withdraw from the present. Negation denotes, therefore, the human refusal to be completely determined by present circumstances. Negation as an experience of absence is one of the major concerns of *Being and Nothingness*.

---

15 Ibid., p. 155.
16 Sartre, *Critique*, pp. 157, 179.

Time and freedom: The existential experience of absence

The concept of absence prefaces the entire work of *Being and Nothingness* and refers to the human capacity to formulate questions or to harbor desires with respect to entities that are not present. "I arrive at the café a quarter of an hour late. Pierre is always punctual. Will he have waited for me? I look at the room, the patrons and I say, 'He is not here' . . . It is an objective fact at present that I have *discovered* this absence, and it presents itself as a synthetic relation between Pierre and the setting in which I am looking for him. Pierre's absence haunts this café and is the condition of its 'self-nihilating' organization as ground." [17] There is a social experience of the "not" which is a form of objective sorting and classification. It occurs as a sudden break in the continuity of certain types of experience when one becomes conscious of a lack or of non-being.

The capacity to experience absence is also the capacity to "annihilate" the "presently given" or to withdraw from it. The "given" becomes suspended between "being" and "nothingness." We are conscious of an absence as a lack in our lives. This does not mean that absence resides in consciousness as a "thing"; instead, it occurs when the experience of the "not" becomes consciousness itself. Thus, the capacity to experience absence appears as an original condition of consciousness itself. This is the condition which is the root of all philosophical and scientific inquiry. Ordinary, everyday human experiences of absence or nothingness are experiences of regret, hatred or prohibition. These are the negative experiences of the *Dasein* in Heidegger's work.

The questioner, by questioning, or the desiring person, by experiencing a lack or absence, is really disengaging himself from the weight of the present, and is thus temporarily not subject to the given order of things. "Thus in posing a question, a certain negative element is introduced into the world. We see

[17] Sartre, *Being and Nothingness*, pp. 40–42. The term "self-nihilation" refers to the disappearance from my field of awareness of all objects, faces, voices, and so on that are not Pierre.

nothingness making the world iridescent, casting a shimmer over things." [18] Consciousness, by way of experiencing an absence or by way of questioning a state of being, is the activity of withdrawing from the present and annihilating it. Such a type of activity is a permanent human possibility, allowing us to wrench ourselves away from the presently given determinants. This wrenching away from being, which is effected in order to bring about the possibility of a different reality, is an objective behavior and not necessarily a subjective attitude of reflection. By experiencing lack or negativity I have a permanent tool for disengagement, by the exercise of which I can "be out of reach." This human relation to the world, however, can never be that of total withdrawal from it; the totality of being cannot even provisionally be suspended. The person's relation with being is that he can modify it.

Since it is oriented toward a goal, human action is oriented toward a possibility in the future. Goals are distant from the present. It is precisely their distance which "casts a shimmer over things." The present becomes vulnerable and its determinations somehow neutralized. The absent goal, toward which an action is oriented, should not be understood as an abstraction. It has objective and tangible effects. Only through positing a future goal can the present world be judged, for example, as good or evil, or can the present social arrangement appear as an obstacle or as an aid. The positing of goals, even at the level of mere *desire,* is one of the sources of social values and judgment.

Freedom and anguish

A person may have negative attitudes not only toward the social world, but also toward himself. This is the foundation for Sartre's two basic principles of human ontology, *pour-soi* and *en-soi* (the "for-itself" and the "in-itself"), which are found throughout *Being and Nothingness,* but have not been discarded in his later work. They were reintroduced in the *Critique,*

[18] Ibid., p. 58.

with even greater insight, as the principles not only of individual action but also of collective human engagements in society and history. The two are joint concepts, mutually defining one another. They represent the dialectics of human work on matter, as well as of human relationships. *Pour-soi* and *en-soi* stand for the duality of the person as an acting agent and as an agent being acted upon.

Human consciousness is not a thing which first exists and then desires this or that. By Sartre's view, human consciousness first exists as a desire or lack. In every attempt to comprehend the Self, we see it as incomplete, as a "wanting being." This is the basic characteristic of the *pour-soi* or the for-itself or consciousness. Consciousness, in general, is a desire for "things"; it is at all times aware of an object, with the realization that it can never coincide with that thing which it desires or with that which it is conscious of. Thus, consciousness possesses no fixed or permanent attributes except its desire for the "thing," "object" or "being," which exists outside of it. Humanity creates its own products but it can never coincide with them, since it is forever condemned to go beyond them. "Human reality is a perpetual surpassing toward a coincidence with itself which is never given." [19] Humanity is always *distanced* from its own creations. This distance is also the distinctive characteristic of its freedom. Thus, consciousness cannot exhaust itself by way of an accomplished arrangement in the world, such as "role," "position," "identity" and so forth. It is always oriented toward absence. Consciousness is a nothingness in pursuit of being or value, but it never corresponds to this or that being or value. This also accounts for its attributes of restlessness, movement or temporality; it always veers toward a state which is not present, that is, toward a possibility. Thus, consciousness or the for-itself is driven toward what it is not, always maintaining a distance between it and its given state of being, constraints, structures, obstacles and so on. Since it is a mere desire or lack, and because it is not a fixed attribute with a certain nature, consciousness as the for-itself is also characterized by Sartre as

[19] Ibid., p. 139.

nothingness, meaning simply that it is "not a particular object, or a state of being, or a thing."

But the desire of the for-itself (human consciousness) as the "human freedom in search of something" is directed toward the social world. Here, the concept of the social world can appear in the guise of a material condition, state of being, value, identity or what Sartre would refer to as "being-in-itself." Being-in-itself, the concept of *en-soi,* in-itself (mentioned above) constitutes the massive reality around us. The in-itself is what it is in the "absolute fullness of its identity." In contrast to the for-itself, or consciousness, the in-itself possesses no lack or desire. For lack appears in the world only with the "upsurge of the human reality."

Since it exhausts itself in what it is, the in-itself is positivity and it has no tension or inner negation. It is subject to the laws of causality and hence it is unfree. The description of the in-itself is not meant to characterize inert matter or social facts alone. For a social being may also wish to escape his freedom and may begin to operate in the guise of a powerless in-itself, creating a false state of consciousness, using what Sartre refers to as mechanisms of "bad faith."

Consciousness can take upon itself a series of roles, or modes of being; but it never remains fixed into modes of being which it is presently filling since it is condemned to go beyond, in other words, to become what it is not at the present. It distances itself from what it is at the moment. It follows that every act of consciousness is an instance of negation, that is, of breaking away from the in-itself. This is the human structure of freedom, exercised in every act, even though it be of the most ordinary or mundane nature. This human structure is the ability to stand back and categorize the world and the self without permanently being *this* world or *this* self.

In Sartre's existentialism the concept of being, in contrast to consciousness, is an objective reality. It is not a state of mind but a massive world of things and of social facts as they present themselves transphenomenally, that is, as the foundation of all phenomena. The being of an object is therefore more than the perspectives which any consciousness can take toward

it: Sartre is an epistemological realist. In fact, the world or
being overflows the knowledge I can have of it; it is not a
mere creation of my mind. Indeed, analysis of consciousness
itself comes from the dialectic which inextricably connects it
to the world.

In Sartre's work, the concept of freedom takes on two con-
notations which are complementary. In *Being and Nothingness*
freedom is a radical condition resting on the ontological status
of man *qua* man. In the *Critique,* the concept of freedom appears as an historical condition, qualified by the constrictions of
human affiliation, social obligation, material scarcity and so
forth. But common to both usages is the human prerogative for
transcendence, that is, for the surpassing of the given. Transcendence is detachment, but detachment is not retirement from
the world, or a separation from existence, in the manner the
stoical consciousness attains its freedom, for example. On the
contrary, Sartre speaks of detachment as the desire to change the
world: freedom here implies the need to take up an active stance
vis-à-vis the world; it requires praxis. This is why freedom for
Sartre always entails the problem of responsibility. "... [M]an
is condemned to be free. Condemned, because he did not create
himself, yet in other respects is free; because once thrown into
the world he is responsible for everything he does." [20] Nothing
can serve as an excuse for discarding such responsibility, not
even passion, for, according to Sartre, the individual is also responsible for his passions.

The realms of transcendence and of possibility, as aspects of
freedom, are not theoretical; choice is not an attitude of the
mind which would lead to the kind of solipsism of which Sartre
is often incorrectly accused. Possibility, for Sartre, is equivalent
to the risk taken in concrete action. "The moment the possibilities I am considering are not rigorously involved by my action,
I ought to disengage myself from them, because no God, no
scheme, can adapt the world and its possibilities to my will." [21]

[20] Jean-Paul Sartre, *Existentialism and Human Emotions* (New
York: The Wisdom Library, 1957), p. 23.
[21] Ibid., p. 29.

Since human reality has no *a priori* essence, nature or deity to fall back upon, it has no excuses. Humanity is responsible for the product of its actions. Responsibility is overwhelming, since it is by the actions of the human group that there happens to be a world. Sartre holds that the mood which accompanies this realization should be one of optimism, since our destinies are in our own hands and since the relationship between the human participant and the world is one of involvement and action.[22]

The staggering responsibilities of freedom must also create a sense of apprehension, which Sartre calls anguish. Anguish in the broadest sense is the human attitude toward freedom. The attitude is one of both apprehension and exhilaration. Anguish is anguish before myself. Sartre means by this that anguish occurs because I can actively pursue options that are not imposed from the outside or that are not conditioned by the determinants of the in-itself. In his example of a man standing at the edge of a precipice, Sartre says: "Vertigo is anguish to the extent that I am afraid not of falling over the precipice, but of throwing myself over."[23]

Anguish is not fear. Fear is apprehension of a situation acting upon me, while anguish is the apprehension of me acting upon a situation. Fear is therefore an attitude toward the contingencies of the in-itself; it is directed toward the object feared. On the other hand, anguish is anxiety when faced with the possibility of realizing the freedom of one's *pour-soi*. Anguish is, then, a reflective attitude toward my possibilities.

In the affectual realm of daily experience anguish is the attitude of awe which comes about when one faces one's future—as if one had to carve an image upon the void. I experience anguish because *nothingness* separates me from my future or because the given, as the *status quo*, will always have to be surpassed. In this sense, anguish operates not in the guise of anticipating the unknown, but with the knowledge that decisive behavior which will determine my future projects must emanate from a Self which I have not yet become. Sartre convincingly

[22] Sartre, *Being and Nothingness*, p. 65.
[23] Ibid., p. 65.

illustrates this temporal aspect of anguish with an example of somebody awaiting his completed projects in the future. "I make an appointment with myself on the other side of that hour, of that day, or of that month. Anguish is the fear of not finding myself at that appointment, of no longer even wishing to bring myself there." [24]

Anguish and the spirit of seriousness

A subtle sociological aspect of anguish can be found in its relation to social values. In the Weberian framework of analysis the habitual values based on everyday conventions can ordinarily serve as refuge with respect to the problem of anguish. Such mechanisms of escape from anguish are characteristically those of the authoritarian group or individual, who, by force of tradition and inhibited reflection, comes to regard values as absolute and as possessing a transcendent quality of their own. This is the type of social group or individual which is contaminated by what Sartre refers to as the "spirit of seriousness." This term is not particular to Sartre, however, for Nietzsche called it the "spirit of gravity." By this phrase, used in the existential literature, the following is meant (a) conferring more reality on the world (the *en-soi*) than on the human component in it (*pour-soi*), (b) considering the human element as a product of the world and (c) approaching values as absolute and objective entities, independent of human volition.

When governed by the spirit of seriousness, the social group relinquishes responsibility for its human condition and no longer freely ascribes the values it chooses to the products of its actions. In submitting to the significance of values in the inherited tradition and to the hierarchy of the given moral standards, a person avoids responsibility and anxiety. This is why the spirit of seriousness stands in opposition to anguish. "Anguish is opposed to the mind of the serious man who apprehends values in terms of the world and who resides in the reassuring, materialistic substantiation of values. . . . [T]he meaning which my free-

[24] Ibid., p. 73.

dom has given to the world, I apprehend as coming from the world and constituting my obligations." [25]

The spirit of seriousness implies, then, an ethic of helplessness in the face of the inherited moral injunctions of this world. This is characteristic of the totalitarian mentality in its requirement for unquestioning and passive obedience to authority. For Nietzsche and Sartre, as well as for Weber, the analysis of this automatic action constituted a major aspect of their work.[26] All three denounce the spirit of seriousness and favor critical consciousness, a consciousness which is bound to moral choice and which holds itself accountable for the consequences of its own actions. The idea of the spirit of seriousness will be further examined in chapter three as an important factor in Sartre's theory of action.

Voluntarism and valuation in Sartre and Weber

Weber refers implicitly to the moral laziness inherent in traditional behavior, one of the four categories of his typology of social action. He speaks of inherited convention as being devoid of critical evaluation and as something "adhered to through the habituation of long practice." He contrasts this type of social behavior with "value-oriented behavior" and "goal-oriented behavior," two other categories of his typology; these, in contrast to the first type, contain rational and self-conscious formulations of principles governing human action.[27] Value-oriented behavior follows an ethic of conviction, that is, the pursuit of behavior according to ultimate injunctions of a moral, aesthetic, religious or political nature, regardless of cost or consequences. In contrast, goal-oriented behavior is not governed by such values, but by rationally calculated considerations of alternative means to an end in a spirit of marginal utility. Here the ethics of action is the ethics of responsibility, based on consciously planned courses

25 Ibid., p. 78.

26 With respect to Nietzsche, see his sections on "Of the Spirit of Gravity" and "Of Old and New Law Tables" in *Thus Spoke Zarathustra*. Weber addresses it in the analysis of traditional action.

27 Weber, "The Fundamental Concepts of Sociology," pp. 115–18.

of behavior.[28] Though Weber justifies both ethics, his sympathy appears to be for the ethic of responsibility. This admiration for the individual actor who feels obliged to give an account of the consequences of his actions is obvious in what follows:

> I am under the impression that in nine out of ten cases I deal with windbags who do not fully realize what they take upon themselves but who intoxicate themselves with romantic sensations. From a human point of view this is not very interesting to me, nor does it move me profoundly. However, it is immensely moving when a mature man—no matter whether old or young in years—is aware of a responsibility for the consequences of his conduct and really feels such responsibility with heart and soul. He then acts by following an ethic of responsibility and somewhere he reaches the point where he says: 'Here I stand; I can do no other.' That is something genuinely human and moving. And every one of us who is not spiritually dead must realize the possibility of finding himself at some time in that position.[29]

In the last analysis, however, the two rational types of ethics can supplement each other, and for Weber this combination constitutes a genuinely moral individual.

Weber, like Sartre, in maintaining a voluntaristic conception of human behavior, recognizes and defines the relativity and variability of values. In his view, no set of values can claim universal validity or priority. This is why the theme of choice recurs in his work: each of us is obliged to pursue competing and sometimes contending doctrines. For Weber, choice is formulated with a strong sense of its tragic inevitability. The absence of sacred and absolute values as guideposts in this world is an inescapable historical condition of contemporary man. "We cannot evade it [choice] as long as we remain true to ourselves. And if Tolstoi's question recurs to you . . . who is to answer the

28 Max Weber, "Politics as a Vocation," in *From Max Weber*, trans., ed. and with an introduction H. H. Gerth and C. Wright Mills (New York: Oxford University Press), pp. 77–128.
29 Ibid., p. 127.

question: 'What shall we do, and how shall we arrange our lives?' Or, in the words used here tonight: 'Which of the warring gods should we serve? Or should we serve perhaps an entirely different god, and who is he?' Then one can say that only a prophet or a savior can give the answers." [30] According to Weber, "we live in a godless and prophetless time," and history is essentially an endless process of creation and destruction of values. Thus, the task of the student of culture is not merely, in the spirit of seriousness, to trace behavior to external structures. His task is to comprehend the meaning that the social group gives to its own existence.

For Weber, our freedom to choose from among the different gods competing for our souls entails an attitude not merely of hope and of reflection but of engagement and active responsibility. In contrasting the modern man to the biblical person, Weber concludes: ". . . [W]e want to draw the lesson that nothing is gained by yearning and tarrying alone, and we shall act differently. We shall set to work and meet the 'demands of the day,' in human relations as well as in our vocation. This, however, is plain and simple, if each finds and obeys the demon who holds the fibers of his very life." [31]

The human condition, for Sartre and for Weber, refers, then, to the condition of the person who acts as a conscious "valuator." Valuation, as the human prerogative, had already been stressed by Nietzsche, as that attitude and approach to the world which can redeem us from modern nihilism. But this privileged condition of valuation is diminished with the rise of the positivistic mentality and with the increasing acceptance of impersonal structures as explanatory of human behavior. These trends are not acceptable to either Weber or Sartre since both regard the analysis of impersonal forces as leading to an unintelligible or misleading type of knowledge.

It is interesting to note Weber's attitude toward theories of psychological determination centering around concepts of the

[30] Max Weber, "Science as a Vocation," in *From Max Weber*, pp. 152–53.
[31] Ibid., p. 156.

irrational or unconscious mind. Gerth and Mills observe that although Weber developed the concept of charisma, he resisted the notion of viewing the personality as an unintelligible and irrational entity: "Weber sees in the concept of 'personality' a much-abused notion referring to a profoundly irrational center of creativity, a center before which analytical inquiry comes to a halt." [32] Weber contends that the unit of analysis in the social sciences should be the understandable behavior of the person. The attempt can be made to interpret one's behavior as well as the behavior of the other in the light of rational relations of ends and means. Considering human valuation as a crucial element of human ends is the interpretive mode of analysis in the human sciences. "[B]y emphasizing the understandability of human conduct, as opposed to the mere causal explanation of 'social facts' as in natural science, Weber draws the line between his interpretive sociology and the 'physique sociale' in the tradition of Condorcet, which Comte called *sociologie* and Durkheim worked out in such an eminent manner." [33]

Sartre, just as Weber, criticizes modes of causal explanation found in determinism, whether such methods be used in psychology or sociology. In Sartre's opinion, determinism is a conscious defense against intelligible modes of explanation, and thus against man's responsibility for his "made world." Determinism gives us a fixed nature which is held to be the cause of our acts, and it treats man as a mere thing. It mires our actions in inertia and externality, thereby reducing us, in Sartre's words, *"to never being anything but what we are,* it reintroduces in us the absolute positivity of being-in-itself and thereby reinstates us at the heart of being." [34] Its evil rests in denying us the freedom of exercising a willed life.

The "unconscious," for Sartre, is an example of internal determinism, which disguises anguish by annihilating the possibilities of the subject. It turns the intelligible sense of responsibility into an amorphous feeling of helplessness and anxiety. In light

[32] Gerth and Mills, *From Max Weber*, p. 55.
[33] Ibid., p. 57.
[34] Sartre, *Being and Nothingness*, pp. 78–79.

of such psychological structures, one's particular possibility becomes the possibility of an undifferentiated "other." That "other" is the "every other" who acts in the same manner under identical circumstances. Thus, in this mode of interpretation, comprehension of the self is accomplished from "without," as is the comprehension of "every other," or as is the comprehension of a thing.

A sociology which would be intelligible would approach social structures and facts as products of human praxis. Indeed, both Weber and Sartre are of the view that adequate sociological investigation should trace abstract institutions to their grounding in human values and praxis. What appears at first as an objective process, a thing-among-things divorced from human intentions or goals, is actually the consequence of a previous set of human projects. Behind orders of society and continuities in history stands a human value or praxis.

For Sartre and Weber the world is constituted by two dimensions of being: matter and consciousness, or things and human values. The world of things is externally determined by causal laws. The world of consciousness, on the other hand, resists such determination. Any attempt to reduce the one to the other is an act of bad faith.

The person is both his given situation *and* his open possibilities (*en-soi* and *pour-soi*); the person is more than merely "what is happening to him," and in this sense is both constrained *and* free. The person is both facticity and transcendence. But in bad faith the person cancels one or another of the dimensions of being, thus denying their constant interplay. The cancelling of transcendence or of facticity can take several paths. What is common to all of them is that they falsely obviate both anguish and the demands for making a choice, that is, for valuation, a prerequisite for authentic and critical humanness.

The concept of bad faith

While the term *bad faith* may sound all-encompassing, it actually applies to specific aspects of human thinking and behavior which will be investigated below.

The experience and exercise of freedom and choice is an experience of responsibility which can therefore entail anguish. A person attempts to flee from responsibility and from anguish by using what Sartre calls "patterns of bad faith." These patterns are mental and behavioral mechanisms which place the person at a distance from his real condition as a free being, and they disengage one's consciousness from the awareness of one's possibilities. Bad faith can take several paths. Analysis of the primary ones is relevant. These categories of bad faith are ideal types and the person's behavior may approximate but does not completely exhaust their features. Also, the person may use more than one of these categories in daily life.

The positivistic solution. By use of this pattern of bad faith the person turns himself into a mere thing; and assumes himself to be compelled to act in certain ways by forces beyond his control. In this case he considers himself a thing-in-itself, an object determined by objective external forces, be they education, background, race, sex, or other factors. The person renounces autonomy and responsibility and levels his own freedom by giving it over to inert environmental circumstance, to his biological organism, or to his "essential nature." Here, there is a denial of possibility and transcendence; the individual becomes the sum total of "what is happening to him." This is also the maner in which positivistic sociology and psychology tend to explain human behavior.

The stoical solution. By appropriating this type of bad faith (in contrast to the first category) the person turns himself into pure consciousness. He pretends to be freedom alone, uninfluenced by facts and events occurring in his surroundings. An interesting example of such a solution is given by Sartre. He discusses a woman attempting to separate her Self from her body in order to live solely as the intellectual being. "But then suppose [her companion] takes her hand. This act of her companion risks changing the situation by calling for an immediate decision. . . . We know what happens next; the young woman leaves her hand there, but she *does not notice* that she is leaving it . . . she is at this moment all intellect . . . she shows herself in her essential aspect—a personality, a consciousness . . . neither consenting nor resisting—a thing." [35] The stoical solution often applies to types of behavior less casual than this example given by Sartre. For the oppressed or the disaffected, the flight to pure consciousness, to the realm of mere thoughts, can mean a separation from the pains and suffering of existence. This solution is not only typical for the individual person, but it also influences the group as a whole, once the group apprehends itself as locked into an insufferable and oppressive historical reality.

The ontological solution. This solution is found in the person who totally identifies himself with a given social role. He becomes nothing else but what he is expected to be, unwaveringly loyal to fixed modes of conduct and judgment imposed from above and without. The expectations of others actually become his desires, and almost come to constitute his own nature. By realizing a role the person feels that he is "living up" to his own true nature. But since Sartre denies any fixed or specific nature or "essence," the person can never really actualize a specified human nature, unless it be in bad faith.

For Sartre, the person is always what *he is not*. The person does not possess a determined nature or a fixed self that can be actualized. The person is fundamentally a "flight toward . . ." possibilities which are never constant or certain. Self-actualization is thus a contradiction in terms since one's action can never coincide with one's "nature." My action defines my nature and not vice versa (or, "existence precedes essence"). Sartre denies an *a priori* human nature that is the property of everyone. Hence, for Sartre, there is no one path which leads to the "right life" or which points to a universal condition of well-being. To speak of a fixed innate nature is to speak of prior determinants which contradict the notion of freedom.

The traditional solution. This kind of bad faith occurs when the individual acts in a spirit of seriousness (discussed above), when he unthinkingly takes traditional judgment as transcendent and non-problematic truth. This is the state of affairs where the person unquestioningly accepts the values of the given world, that is, of the structure, object or accomplished deed, as

[35] Ibid., p. 97.

independent of human significations. It is the mode of behavior closest to traditional action in Weberian typology.

Conditions which are conducive to bad faith traverse daily existence and are not peculiar to any single type or group of people. Sartre does not give a pathological or irrational connotation to the phenomenon of bad faith. The person often uses bad faith consciously, instead of unconsciously, since a lie, for Sartre, must always have a liar. The triunal interplay of "freedom/anguish/bad faith" is not a philosophical artifact or a metaphysic. We habitually avoid the "demands of the day" by not taking up choices, and by trying to ward off responsibility through deceptive rationalizations.

two

Relationships

with the

other

The problem of identity in Mead and Sartre

A great deal of discomfort can be involved in the fact that there is no fixed human nature as such, and that one cannot appropriate a permanent identity. The Self, Sartre implies, does not endure in strict correspondence with the consciousness one has of it. The choice made in the present with respect to the future cannot guarantee that the same choice will be repeated again in the future. There is no fully determined relationship between the Self as given in the present and its future projects. This is so because each "act goes farther than the self." [1] What determines the enduring quality of a present project with respect to the future is not the structure and nature of the self as such (ontology) but the force of morality, of habit, of daily custom and of social obligation, that is, of one's sociality. In this connection it is important to say that ontology and sociality are often not capable of being harmonized. In fact, the person violates the reality of the one by realizing the demands of the other. Radical freedom, as a structure of my ontology, for example, is limited by the actuality of my social projects. The interplay between ontology and sociality is the perpetual dilemma of the individual and the collective, with which the major social theorists, from Durkheim to the

[1] Jean-Paul Sartre, *Being and Nothingness,* trans. Hazel E. Barnes (New York: Washington Square Press, 1973), p. 82.

present time, have dealt in one manner or another. In *Being and Nothingness* Sartre does not treat this dilemma expressly, unless we, when reading this work, equate sociality with the concept of the *en-soi.* The dilemma reappears in his *Critique,* where it receives a more explicit and programmatic analysis.

Sartre's analysis of the present identity of the Self which is at odds with the future project is reminiscent of Mead's work on the same problem in *Mind, Self and Society.* Mead differentiates two aspects of the Self: the "Me" and the "I." The Me is the conventional social component of the Self. It consists of the attitudes of others and contains habitual attitudes which prepare the person to act in a predictable manner. Thus, one's education and socialization constitute the Me as a unified and stable self. But Mead, unlike Durkheim, does not stop his analysis there. For over and against the habitualized Me stands the I, the innovative and creative component of this Self. While the Me conditions one's attitudes and choices, it cannot fully determine what action will be taken. One is never certain how one will act, Mead tells us, until the act has been accomplished. Every present act is unique and cannot be absolutely predetermined by one's perceived identity. In Mead's words, "it is because of the 'I' that we say that we are never fully aware of what we are, that we surprise ourselves by our own actions. It is as we act that we are aware of ourselves." [2]

The future response of the I is always uncertain for Mead, since it is neither calculable nor social. The Me-identity prepares the person to meet the obligations of his social reality, but the I is always something different from what that reality calls for. The Self is essentially made up of these two distinctive phases: "If it [the Self] did not have these two phases, there could not be conscious responsibility and there would be nothing novel in experience." [3]

Generally speaking, the concept of the I is similar to the Sar-

[2] George H. Mead, *Mind, Self and Society,* ed. with an introduction by Charles W. Morris (Chicago: The University of Chicago Press, 1962), p. 174.
[3] Ibid., p. 178.

trean concept of transcendence, or the structure of the *pour-soi,* which is not determined causally. The I reveals itself in the performed act and defies all prior reflection and judgments about it. But unlike Sartre, Mead attempts to bring about a reconciliation between ontology and sociality. The Me stands for the common and social aspects of the person while the I represents the possibility for unique differences among actors. For Mead, both take part in the formation of social processes. The Me represents habitual and obligatory aspects of social life and includes no moral urgency, tension or risk. Understandably, this is why the act of calling upon the attitudes of the Me is the calling for socially legitimated certainty and approval. One may add that the Me is the only Self of which one is habitually aware. The Me is the Self which exists in the context of the group's valuation of it. "To be a 'me' under those circumstances [of group approval] is the important thing. It gives [the person] his position, ... the dignity of being a member of the community, [and] it is the source of his emotional response to the values that belong to him as a member of the community." [4]

A rigid adherence to the socialized self produces inertia which is reminiscent of the dimension of the *en-soi.* But such inertia not only characterizes the bad faith of an individual Me, but also the bad faith contained in certain systems of knowledge. This is true, for example, about positivism as a mode of analysis. In the spirit of "physical engineering," positivistic analysis in the social sciences levels down the attributes of the Self to those of matter and offers us a sociology of "things." It instills in the human being a feeling of helplessness and gross inferiority *vis-à-vis* the world, since it considers the Self to be the passive product of unintelligible structures and conceives of the human group as immutable, as containing only fixed and unchanging attributes capable of being predicted and controlled. The idea of the Me becomes a fixed "nature" or "essence," related only to its past. "Essence is all that human reality apprehends in itself as *having been.*" This is why the positivistic mentality resists the notion of *making the Self,* since the making of the Self is

[4] Ibid., p. 199.

what designates a free being, described by Mead as being capable of innovation and surprise. The positivistic mentality escapes the anguish of having to make the Self by preconstituting the priority of the environment, or by making claims about "essential humanity." This escape amounts to investing one's freedom in a completely abstract or brutishly inanimate dimension. But in either case one does realize that the origin of this external determination is humanity itself. It is I, says Sartre, who invests the situation or the Other with values, whereby they appear as an obstacle or an aid in relation to my projects. "My indignation has given to me the negative value 'baseness,' my admiration has given the positive value 'grandeur.' " [5] With the realization that it is only through me that values exist and receive their hierarchy, there remains little justification in selecting this or that scale of values. This does not lead to nihilism however, but to a heightened consciousness of the responsibility involved in being a valuator. Bad faith attempts to circumvent the claims of my human responsibility as a decision-maker. Its devices of avoidance are the same as those of the positivistic mentality which derives satisfaction from disarming human freedom.

To overcome bad faith, in life as in knowledge, is to reach the realization that my facticity and my freedom, the Me and the I are interconnected. Matter and consciousness are merged in a process of mutual signification. One cannot be authentic by dissociating oneself from the contingencies of the in-itself, nor by submitting to it totally. Human reality is a dual process of action and inertia (or praxis and seriality in the *Critique*), of choice and routinization, of being a *pour-soi* and of being an *en-soi*. The actualization of the one cannot escape the consequences of the other.

The human capacity for being and transcendence stands at odds with our convention of "sincerity." Sartre uses the concept of sincerity not as a moral idea but as a fixation in behavior. For Sartre, the goal of sincerity is no different from some of the patterns of bad faith, since to be sincere means to be in constant loyalty to the same Self, a characteristic of the Me or the in-

---

[5] Sartre, *Being and Nothingness,* pp. 72, 76.

itself. Inhering in the "sincere Self" is a principle of identity stifling the human activity of negation and change. It suggests an equivalence between facticity and transcendence, which is an impossibility for Sartre. Human reality can never realize itself in one continuous role or identity. "I am never any one of my attitudes, any one of my actions." Even when I am situated in the psychic attitude of sadness as it is given in my depression, I do not hold to this attitude permanently, says Sartre. It is not an uncontrollable passion but a certain chosen behavior. The person appears helplessly caught by the attitude but "[l]et a stranger suddenly appear and I will lift up my head, I will assume a lively cheerfulness. What will remain of my sadness except that I obligingly promise it an appointment for later. . . . Is not this sadness itself a conduct?" [6] Whatever behavioral role or emotional attitude I adopt, I adopt it consciously and temporally, almost as though it were a game between my givenness and my possibilities. Sartre is speaking of sincerity as an ontological attitude, as a permanent identity, a fixed Self, or a human nature. Sincerity requires that the Self be constituted as a thing. As one commentator put it: "Indeed, we are aware that what is usually described as sincerity is, in fact, bad faith, for it is an attempt to escape the constant obligation of becoming and to rest in a state of stability." [7]

The Other in Hegel, Sartre and Mead

In addition to the two modes of being, for-itself and in-itself, *pour-soi* and *en-soi*, there is for Sartre a third mode of being: being-for-the-Other.

Sartre's analysis of the Other is among the richest of the themes which he treats in *Being and Nothingness*. His philosophical analysis merges with an analysis of routine and mundane reality of daily life. In fact, the potential of this analysis is so powerful that Sartre expands upon it in the *Critique* so that

---

[6] Ibid., pp. 103, 104.

[7] Joseph S. Catalano, *A Commentary on Jean-Paul Sartre's Being and Nothingness* (New York: Harper Torchbooks, 1974), p. 85.

the ontological analysis develops into an historical one. Encounters between individual selves become group relations. He develops a theory concerning the genesis of the group with its attendant realities—that is, of pledge and deflection, revolt and routinization—which will be analyzed in later chapters.

In his treatment of the Other, Sartre was undoubtedly influenced by Hegel's theory of self-consciousness (*Phenomenology of Mind,* the section "Lordship and Bondage"). Hegel's powerful thesis had also deeply influenced Marx. But despite Sartre's criticisms of Hegel's theory of self-consciousness (which is also a theory of the Other) Sartre refers to Hegel's idea as a "brilliant intuition" and creatively expands upon it and reworks it.[8] On the other hand, the contributions made by Kant and Husserl with respect to the theory of the Other are discarded, since, in his view, both these philosophers envision a connection between Self and Other which can be realized only through knowledge. In the context of their philosophy, the problem of the existence of the Other is part of the problem of the existence of the world in general. According to them, the *existence* of the Other as part of the world can be affirmed only through the *knowledge* which one has of the Other and of the world. Sartre rejects the thought as a perverted attempt to measure existence by knowledge, because existence precedes the knowledge we have of it. Hegel, in contrast, established the fact that the Other is not only constitutive of the truth of the existence of the world, but also of self-consciousness itself. It is through the Other that I apprehend myself. The Other mediates my self-awareness, and one would risk his very life, as Hegel puts it, in order to gain the Other's recognition.

Ontologically, the Other appears as an alien freedom, as the upsurge of another subjectivity with its own consciousness as well as with its own desire for a human world. Any ontological encounter with it is grounded in a spirit of alarm since the Other and the Self compete in their mutual desires for the human world. On the historical level, the encounter ushers in the various regimes of human history, that is, those based on the

[8] Sartre, *Being and Nothingness,* pp. 320–30.

acceptance of the Other as an independent freedom, as opposed to those which instead refuse him and thereby subjugate him. Empirically, the relationship between Self and Other has predominantly occurred in the latter mode. This conflict mode between Self and Other characterizes the works of both Hegel and Sartre. Thus, Sartre rejects the view which Heidegger adopts, namely, that coexistence, the *mit-sein,* is the foundation for the relationship between Self and Other. This "being-with," while it characterizes the structure of "being-in-the-world" as coexistence, can by no means explain the coming into being of my concrete relations with the Other, nor can it resolve the problem of the recognition of the Other. Sartre insists that "we *encounter* the Other; we do not constitute him." [9] This is so because the Other is an independent *pour-soi,* an "irreducible fact." But let us remember, it was Hegel who discovered the concepts, developed the dialectic, and paved the way for any significant discussion in which the Other is seen to be the basis for the problem of domination in human history. Both Marx and Sartre criticized and transformed Hegel's theory of the Other, yet they remained essentially indebted to it.

Master-slave relationship

Hegel begins his analysis with the idea that the Self does not know the Other as it knows itself and hence works toward the mediation of the Other. That is to say, one seeks to comprehend the Other not through the immediacy of the Other's presence (as existence) but through his mediated activity (e.g., as a worker, as a teacher, as an artist, and so forth). Hence, the comprehension of consciousness is not the product of mere contemplation, but a praxis. Consciousness is the way in which a person works on matter. Self-consciousness comes into being when one appears before the Other as acting agent. The person becomes conscious of his identity as maker of the world before the Other.

The immediate structure of consciousness is desire. In this connection, desire is a "gap" between the world as it is and the

[9] Ibid., pp. 334, 336.

world as it ought to be. The desire of human consciousness is to change the world and to create a different human condition. For Hegel, however, consciousness becomes self-consciousness not merely through impersonal transformation of the world, but by being recognized in the act of transforming the world. Self-consciousness denotes the awareness existing between two mutually desirous consciousnesses of their struggle for each other's acknowledgment: Self-consciousness "comes about only by being acknowledged or recognized." Recognition of the Other is not an existential event, given in terms of experiencing him as "bare existence," but is an historical event, given in terms of facing the Other as an agent in the world devising its own freedom. This freedom is most exercised where the Other even risks life. In Hegel's words: "[T]he individual, who has not staked his life, may no doubt, be recognized as a person; but he has not attained the truth of this recognition as an independent self-consciousness." [10]

The struggle between two consciousnesses can end up in the destruction of one of them, but such an act is irrelevant here since it eliminates recognitions altogether. Hence, the solution of the problem of the Other in history has come to mean not "the war of all against all," but the division of humanity into two groups: one which receives recognition and another which confers it, or, more simply put, a division into masters and slaves. "The one is independent, and its essential nature is to be for itself; the other is dependent and its essence is life or existence for another. The former is the master, or Lord, the latter the Bondsman." [11]

The slave, or submissive Other, objectifies himself through serving the master in labor. But in labor, the slave is in touch with the world of things; he acts on the natural world. It is in this context that work mediates between slave and master. In fact the master relates to the world only through the slave's product. He relates to the world as a consuming desire.

[10] G. W. F. Hegel, *The Phenomenology of Mind,* trans. with an introduction and notes by J. B. Baillie (New York: Humanities Press, 1949), second edition, pp. 229, 233.

[11] Ibid., p. 234.

While the master gains recognition, he also realizes that he is a dependent instead of an independent being, since it is the slave who achieves independence. The slave actively recreates himself through work: "[T]he consciousness that toils and serves accordingly attains by this means the direct apprehension of that independent being as its self." [12] In the work which he does, the slave rediscovers himself as the more progressive of the two. He gains self-consciousness by satisfying the needs of the master through labor, that is, through self-objectification.

This relationship of master and slave serves as an historical prototype of human domination. But in reading Hegel's section on "Lordship and Bondage" one surrenders to the insight, first elaborated by Kojève, that it is the slave who moves humanity forward. Work, as his primary relation to nature, gives him immediate access to the cultural and technical world, making him the support of civilization. Mark Poster, in his analysis of Kojève's contribution, sums this up eloquently:

> The slave produced and the master consumed. The slave labored without gratification, while the master's slightest whim was fulfilled without effort. The slave was compelled to delay and to sublimate his desires. The worker thus became civilized or bourgeois, learning to control and direct his desires and in the process achieving control over nature. Subjectively, the working slave learned to marshal and concentrate his energies toward ends that he himself defined, while objectively he created products that confirmed his internal aims and submitted nature to his control.[13]

For Hegel, the meeting of person and person occurs from the "outside" through mediation of labor. There can be no direct meeting between two consciousnesses. The subject can be known only through his dialectical transformations in society. We meet each other in our externalized roles as agents of labor. This is why self-objectification for Hegel is also the source of aliena-

12 Ibid., p. 238.
13 Mark Poster, *Existential Marxism in Postwar France: From Sartre to Althusser* (Princeton: Princeton University Press, 1975), p. 14.

tion. The mediations of consciousness exist as different modes of labor (the physical mode, the intellectual mode, the artistic mode, the religious mode, and so on), conforming to the various stages of historical development. This is so because mediation, through elements of reflection, planning and postponement, comes to enhance awareness in contrast to that state of "bare existence" which characterizes pre-reflective being. This is probably why Hegel looked at the mediated relationship of citizen and state as more progressive than the simple family relationship based on a natural and non-mediated form of affiliation.

It was Sartre's insistence on conflict as the permanent modality of interaction of Self and Other that led him to criticize Hegel's thesis. Hegel's theory is optimistic, Sartre states, for in the long run it resolves the opposition between Self and Other which comes about with reciprocal recognition. At our stage of historical development such a harmonizing of relations between master and slave is absent; but it can be attained, Hegel implied, as an historical possibility.

Sartre appears to rule out the possibility of any direct cognitive relationship between consciousnesses: "[T]he *for-itself* as for-itself cannot be known by the Other. The object which I apprehend under the name of the Other appears to me in a radically *other* form. The Other is not a *for-itself* as he appears to me; I do not appear to myself as I am *for-the-Other*. I am incapable of apprehending for myself the self which I am for the Other." [14] But this is hardly a criticism, since Hegel would agree with Sartre's idea that we come to know, and relate to, and appraise each other as agents of labor, through the manner in which we mediate or transform ourselves into our various and shifting social roles. We are socially affiliated but ontologically separated. This is the dilemma, reappearing again, between sociality and ontology which we encountered earlier.

Sartre also criticizes Hegel on the grounds that Hegel deals with consciousnesses as strictly equivalent to each other, since Hegel's interest is in the truth of the whole, within which these consciousnesses are only empirical moments. Hegel is attempt-

[14] Sartre, *Being and Nothingness*, p. 327.

ing to surpass the plurality of different consciousnesses toward intersubjective totality. Sartre resists this, however: "No logical or epistemological optimism can cover the scandal of the plurality of consciousnesses . . . [for] so long as consciousnesses exist, the separation and conflict of consciousnesses will remain." In Sartre's view, Husserl failed in his analysis of the Other since he measured being by knowledge, and Hegel failed since he identified knowledge with being. This is so even though Sartre admits that "Hegel . . . has been able to put the discussion on its true plane." [15]

Until we reach a different stage in history, the characteristic relationship between consciousnesses will remain that of conflict. On this point Hegel and Sartre agree. Sartre also agrees with the concept of mediation, and he is in accord with Hegel when Hegel maintains that we cannot meet each other directly.

The look: the objectification of Self and Other

To be recognized by the Other, in Sartre's view, is to be an object for the Other. The Other recognizes me only in my externalized role as an object; an object for *his* value judgments. The objectification of me by the Other is dramatized by Sartre by his concept of the "look." "Thus being *seen* constitutes me as a defenseless being for a freedom which is not my freedom. It is in this sense that one can consider ourselves as slaves in so far as we *appear* to the Other" [16] (emphasis mine).

Sartre emphasizes "appearance" instead of "function" as the center of his analysis. He admits that at this stage of his work his description of the human encounter is existential rather than historical and thinks that the slave-master relationship can never be overcome. It is the permanent phenomenology of being-for-Other: "I am a slave to the degree that my being is dependent at the center of a freedom which is not mine and which is the very condition of my being." [17] However, the rest

15 Ibid., pp. 329, 330.
16 Ibid., p. 358.
17 Ibid.

of Sartre's analysis of the Other surprisingly shifts from merely being based on ontology to being founded on cultural and social contexts with an emphasis on social psychology reminiscent of Mead's.

The Other, for Sartre, not only appraises me as an object but eventually establishes in me a new being which self-reflectively passes judgments on myself as object. My shame and pride are modes of being from the vantage point of this Other. Mead also posits such a principle, whereby the other constitutes the Self as object. For Mead, too, it is from the standpoint of other individuals that the person experiences himself as object. The person does not experience life directly or immediately, but through the mediation of the Other. Because the Other is a permanent structure of mediation, existence ceases to be "bare existence" and becomes an area of social and moral life. The person appropriates the attitudes of Others in order to become a Self. For Mead, in fact, there is no possibility of conceiving the Self apart from the social experience with the Other. Thus, self-consciousness, for him, is "the taking or feeling of the attitude of the other toward yourself . . . and not mere organic sensations of which the individual is aware and which he experiences." [18] The social bond between myself and the Other is established through the Other's acts of constituting the Self as Me which is an object for this Other. Likewise, for Sartre and Mead, the Me is my "outside," the property of the Other. It is through this objective, impersonal part of the Self, constituted by generalized attitudes of social experience, that the Other limits and controls it. For Sartre the Me is both a moral and physical entity. In the latter sense, it is best reflected in the concept of the body.

Sociological analysis often portrays the Self as a final, unified product with closed boundaries, and this resembles Sartre's description of the in-itself. But the credibility with which such a finalized Self would take up roles as its own is artificial and has little foundation. It was Goffman who detected the falsity of these sociological views, pointing out the vulnerability of such finalized Selves; they are both existentially and morally vulner-

[18] Mead, *Mind, Self and Society*, pp. 171–72.

able because they are apt to "cave in" with the slightest questioning of what they take for granted.

Durkheim originally conceived of the Self as a fixed identity by seriously considering it to be the extension of the collective conscience. According to him, the Self is the sum total of traditions, habits, customs, and so forth. Mead differs a great deal from Durkheim, and his concept of the I would be anathema to Durkheim's static conception of the person. Nevertheless, Mead is still locked into his view of the Self as a Me, as a closed system of conduct, which is unreflective and loyal to its social origins.

Taking, for example, the shameful, jealous or prideful Self, Mead would consider these attitudes to be cognitive. A person is ashamed of himself from the moral point of view of the Other, which point of view becomes his own morality. This means that the person is instantly shameful in all cases of wrongdoing. He has internalized the Other, which means that the Other does not necessarily have to be present in order for him to experience shame. Also, in him there is hardly any conflict or tension between being and knowing. There is no developmental aspect to his shame; no temporality, moment of emergence, context, and so forth. If we compare Mead to Sartre on this point we find that Sartre would be quick to differentiate between a phase of being which precedes the attitude of shame and a phase of being which constitutes the onset of the feeling of shame as a cognitive state. This point is to be explained by differentiating between *non-thetic* and *reflective* consciousness. In a state of jealousy, for example, my consciousness is said to be non-thetic, meaning that it is unreflective, that is, it is the very act of wanting to hear a conversation or "to see a spectacle." In the non-thetic condition, there is no Self to fall back upon. There is no cognitive point of mediation, for "[m]y consciousness sticks to my acts, it *is* my acts; . . .[m]y attitude . . . has no 'outside'; it is a pure process of relating the instrument (the keyhole) to the end to be attained (the spectacle to be seen)." This is a phase of behavior which precedes cognitive awareness of the Other. At this stage, one's act is not known to the Other, and thus the Other does not yet constrain the

Self. In one's non-thetic experience of the world, the world appears to be constituted by possibilities which are devoid of the transcending view of the Other. In the non-thetic consciousness, everything around the Self relates to its free projects and possibilities. With respect to Sartre's treatment of jealousy: "Jealousy, as the possibility which I *am,* organizes this instrumental complex by transcending it toward itself. But I *am* this jealousy; I do not know it." [19]

But if suddenly footsteps are heard, one's complete structure of consciousness changes. One suddenly sees oneself as an object for reflective consciousness. A self comes to haunt what was previously non-thetic or non-reflective consciousness. "I see myself because *somebody* sees me," and this Self is now the direct object of my consciousness. Thus ". . . the person [Self] is presented to consciousness *in so far as the person is an object for the Other."* Now, my foundation is external. In fact, my situation flows in the direction of the Other, and I become an in-itself for him, an in-itself which closes in upon my freedom. "For the Other *I am leaning over* the keyhole as this tree is bent by the wind. Thus for the Other I have stripped myself of transcendence." [20] The world now centers around the Other, as a hole toward which the entire universe goes. Things no longer have a singular relation to the Self. This is how Sartre concludes his analysis.

The dialectics of objectification between Self and Other which conceptually originated in the master-slave relation are also directed by Sartre to the domains of love and hate. First, he realizes, after the work of Hegel, that consciousness or the *pour-soi* is essentially a *relation.* My freedom does not precede the freedom of the Other but faces it. Secondly, freedom is not completely immune to the presence of the Other. Like the master in Hegel's thesis, Sartre realizes that the Other can conquer me not only through making me dependent on his labor, but also through his love. In the same manner in which the Other can rob me of my independence through love, the Other can

---

[19] Sartre, *Being and Nothingness*, p. 348.
[20] Ibid., pp. 349, 352.

also appropriate my body or destroy it, as happens in the attitude of hate.

With finesse Sartre gives a phenomenological analysis of the
types of relations which the Self can have with the Other (indifference, desire, sadism, and so on). The unifying theme is
that of conflict, which is the basis of all relationships. In this
connection, the attitude of love becomes paradoxical because
no *pour-soi* can directly relate to another *pour-soi,* and the mediation achieved through the body turns the Other into a thing.
Desire fails because it unites one's freedom with another's facticity. An attitude of masochism is another inauthentic attempt
on the part of the Self to relate to the Other; and the sadist
can never vanquish the Other, for the "look" of the victim
establishes the victim's freedom. Through this fascinating analysis Sartre conveys an optimistic, instead of a pessimistic, conviction. This conviction, which runs throughout his work, is that
the Other is essentially a subject, a freedom, a being-for-itself,
which cannot be vanquished. If anything, Sartre sensitizes us to
approach each other as *subjects* approaching *subjects.* One per-
ceives, whether in anxiety or in love, that the possibilities which
one is, belong also to another.

Intimate relationships

Consciousness constitutes a relationship. It is constituted as a
relationship with an Other whose inescapable presence has the
greatest meaning for the Self. This Other judges, confers an
identity and often affirms or denies the freedom of the Self.
In its look, or gaze, the Other reveals its advantage over the
Self. It fashions about the Self a being which the Self cannot
see. "[T]he Other's look fashions my body . . . causes it to be
born, sculptures it, produces it . . . sees it as I shall never see
it. The Other holds a secret—the secret of what I am." The
Other introduces the Self to a state of objectivity while enjoying
the state of consciousness and subjectivity. At the same time
the objectness of the Self in the look of the Other is proof of
the consciousness of the Other, since consciousness is consciousness of an object. The Other "causes me to be." The Self be-

comes a "there is" for the Other. The Self tries to recover the foundation which the Other gives it, but it soon realizes that this is possible only if it transcends and assimilates the freedom of the Other. The foundation of the Self is therefore inextricably bound up with its conflict relation to the Other. "Conflict is the original meaning of being-for-Others." [21] In this connection, each of us is continuously tossed from "being-a-looker" to "being-looked-at," that is to say every person is both freedom and inertia. We are revealed to one another as both subject and object, as *pour-soi* and *en-soi,* or more simply as actors and as those who are acted upon.

The relationship between Self and Other is circular, and equally affects both members of the dyad. It contains many states of being, ranging from love and cooperation to vengeance and destruction. Within the relationship the Self may strive to assimilate the Other's freedom or it may attempt to petrify the Other and turn it into an object. A number of these states of being and attitudinal orientations will be analyzed below.

The love relation. The sociological significance of an analysis of the love relation seems obvious. First, it seems significant since the study of intimate human experiences is rarely taken up by social scientists; second, the analysis clarifies with some examples the basic concepts of *Being and Nothingness;* and third, the material analyzed is particularly instructive when attempting to understand the life of the human group as it is revealed in the *Critique.*

The characteristic of a genuine love relationship, Sartre tells us, is unity in freedom, that is, in the meeting of subjectivities. Each member of the relation desires to maintain his or her individuality even when he or she surrenders to the Other. Each member wishes to strengthen the unity of the members' relatedness as well. But this unity is ideal since a love relation does not completely do away with conflict.

In a love relation it is the freedom of the beloved which is the goal and the foundation of the loving Self. Physical unity by itself will not suffice, since the beloved as consciousness can

21 Ibid., p. 475.

escape the lover even when they are physically bound up with one another. What the Self wishes to assimilate is neither the body nor the facticity of the loved one. Instead it wishes to assimilate the Other as an independent freedom.[22] However, such assimilation is not meant to imply enslavement by either humiliation or compulsion. The lover wants to transform the beloved's freedom from an unpredictable and willful quality into a pledge relationship. It is the pledge which transforms the freedom of the beloved into a bond of love. The Self which loves, however, does not wish to "capture" the Other in any conventional sense. It wishes the "capture" to be willed by the beloved Other. For to merely cause a love relation is to be an instrument which may be discarded or replaced at any time. The lover wants to be a symbol of the whole world for the beloved. The loving Self is willing to be an object in which the beloved Other can lose its freedom. The loving Self yearns to become the objective limit of the beloved's freedom. The freedom of the beloved, upon being encircled by pledge, cannot threaten to transcend the loving Other any more.

In Sartre's mind, the freedom of the beloved, ironically, is a source of alienation for the lover. The lover attempts to seduce this freedom by offering himself as its object of fascination. The beloved's freedom is an alienating agency because it is the beloved who will give meaning to the gestures and expressions of the lover. His language and behavior only reveal to the loving Self the transcendence of the beloved who judges. When the beloved returns love, he does so not because he is fascinated by the loving Self, but since he is willing to appropriate the love offered. He appropriates the love not as body-object but as *freedom*.

The redeeming feature of a love relation is that there exists in the relation a transvaluation of the look or gaze. The gaze of a responsive beloved cannot petrify the lover any longer, since the lover is not an object among objects, but is the foundation through which all other objects are revealed. When transformed by love, the Other's gaze reduces anxiety and in-

22 Ibid., p. 478.

security and turns the Self from an instrument or mere cause into an independent being in the world. The Self suffered before being loved; it suffered its existence as unjustified. But with love requited, unjustifiability is no longer the primary aspect of existence. The joy of love rests in this justification of one's existence. It overcomes estrangement in the world. In his exhilaration the lover relates to the whole world through the beloved. Objects cease to be remote and inert and begin to be sensually perceived. As Sartre puts it: "[T]he warmth of air, the breath of the wind, the rays of sunshine . . . are [thereafter] present[ed] to me in a certain way, as posited upon me without distance and revealing my flesh by means of their flesh." [23]

But this love relation contradicts the ideal of the for-itself. The lover makes the beloved the privileged reference point of his existence; he offers himself as a fascinating object. But when the beloved is seduced and projects back love he also gives back to the lover his "free subjectivity." It is the beloved Other who now "is swallowed up in . . . objectivity" as he faces the loving Self. The responsive beloved returns to the lover his sense of power and autonomy. The two wish to confront each other as though each were an absolute freedom, but such a relation is impossible since subjectivity can found itself only with reference to an object. In Sartre's view, as soon as the beloved loves me he experiences me as subject and falls back into his own objectivity.[24] The resulting disappointment is compounded by the presence of a third party, who, through its judgment and gaze, can petrify the love relation and turn both lovers into mere objects.

The "amorous solution" is therefore doomed. Sartre's point is that love cannot relieve us from the anxiety that accompanies freedom. An attempt to remedy this paradox is made by means of masochism. In the masochistic relation the lover denies his regained subjectivity and refuses to be anything but object. In the masochistic relation the person wishes to become a permanent "being-in-itself" for the Other. His suffering, humiliation

[23] Ibid., p. 509.
[24] Ibid., p. 490.

and shame are the price of his renounced freedom. The difference between the objectivity of the lover in a reciprocal love relation and in a masochistic relation is that, in the first instance, the lover is the subjective limit of the beloved's freedom, while in the second, the lover becomes a mere instrument, an object among objects.[25] The masochist does away with his freedom while wishing the Other's freedom to remain absolute. The masochist does not attempt to seduce the Other or appear to him as a privileged object, but presents himself as a fixed and dead object without even the hope of regaining autonomy. But this relation is also doomed. This is so because no one can really do away with his freedom. The masochist remains aware of the fact that his suffering is contrived. His assumption of the role of a permanent object only heightens his consciousness of his subjectivity. It is this consciousness of his unescapable freedom which gives the anguish he constantly experiences. The Other is *chosen* as a tool to do away with freedom. But one cannot be totally assimilated by the Other. And the pleasure of the masochist is his awareness of his failure to do so.

The idea of desire. The idea of being-for-the-other is the notion of desire itself. For Sartre, desire is not a biological urge that is strictly bound to sexuality. In fact, it precedes the sexual impulse. In desire, the Other is first approached as a mere human being who thereafter reveals that he is a sexed being. For desire does not aim to physically possess the desired object. The proof of this is the fact that the sex act does not eliminate desire. A child can have a desire for another, while being ignorant of the sexual component.

In desiring, one affectually relates to an object which is conscious. The body is never simply desired as body *per se*, but as the embodiment of a type of consciousness. It is consciousness which gives the body its meaning and unity. Desire is thus addressed to another organic being on the unifying ground of the meaning of his consciousness for the Self. The desiring person is a desiring consciousness, a consciousness that longs to submit to facticity in the form of the Other's body. Desire

[25] Ibid., p. 492.

reveals one's own body, not as an instrument, but as facticity, and this facticity troubles consciousness. This is why we think of a desiring consciousness as being opaque. We tend to speak of it as a fact, a datum: "it lives as a burden in us" or "it takes hold of us." "I *feel* my skin and my muscles and my breath . . . as a living and inert datum, not simply as the pliable and discrete instrument of my action upon the world but as a *passion* by which I am engaged in the world. . . ." In desire, consciousness as a for-itself experiences the contingency of its body. The body ceases to be a tool for its projects and becomes an end. In Sartre's terms, "[t]he being which desires is consciousness making itself body." [26]

In the process of desiring an object, consciousness not only appropriates the other as a sensual thing but also appropriates the world as such. It transforms the world and all objects contained in it. It gives them a new point of reference. The world takes on a new meaning which is derived from the point of view of the desiring consciousness. Therefore, the world appears as sensualized facticity.

By approaching the Other, the Self wishes to transform it into facticity. The Self wants to act upon the Other as an object. But the freedom of the Other annihilates the Self's goal and the Other always seems to escape and flee. The Self cannot appropriate the Other's freedom or even grasp it. The Other's reality is beyond the Self's reach. It is the ideal of the for-itself to possess the Other as freedom, but this is only an ideal.

The concept of sadism. The frustration engendered by the Other's freedom may lead to sadism. The sadist desires to strip the Other of his freedom and possibility and "incarnate" him as mere inertia.

Sartre's theory of sadism is situated in an aesthetic theory of the body. The body is said to be in a state of grace when all its parts are adapted to function in harmony with the demands of a situation. A graceful body is one which appears to be a total instrument used to realize a goal called for in the context of the situation. The nudity of a dancer can be called for by a

---

[26] Ibid., p. 505.

certain situation and is, therefore, "graceful," while revealing the body in isolation from the same situation is "obscene." The obscene element in the sadistic relation is that the sadist reveals his victim's body as constituted of isolated parts, and as a thing unrelated to the situation. It is the goal of the sadist to eliminate "grace" from the situation. The Other is made to appear as nothing else but manipulatable flesh, a mere facticity without freedom. The possibilities of the Other are reconstructed to appear as mere acts of compulsion—as automatic reactions to sadistic manipulation.

The sadist experiences himself as total transcendence in the face of the Other as inert flesh. He is desire without opaqueness. His desire appropriates the Other instrumentally while he himself refuses to be appropriated. The sadist conceals his freedom as flesh while enjoying the revealed Other as flesh: "[He] wants the non-reciprocity of sexual relations, [and] enjoys being a free appropriating power confronting a freedom captured by flesh." [27]

But even the sadist realizes that it is only through the Other that his sadism is possible. His aim of taking away the victim's freedom is shattered by the gaze of the victim, a gaze which thwarts the sadist Other.

The conclusion of the discussion of being-for-Other remains consistent with Sartre's central thesis that no person can appropriate the freedom of another. We are denied the ideal of meeting each other as absolute freedoms as well as the goal of totally appropriating each other as instruments. We do not grasp each other directly, but only through the *mediation* of roles, functions and positions in the world. The idea of mediation refers to the idea of *social forms* as objective states of existence. The concept of mediation, therefore, reappears in the *Critique,* taking up broader and richer contexts of social analysis. Sartre follows up the institutional representation of relationships, their ideals and their contradictions, by retracing all social forms back to the concrete interaction of the individual, in whose defense *Being and Nothingness* is written.

27 Ibid., p. 518.

three

The

existential

theory of

action

For Sartre, meaningful action is behavior that is conscious and goal-oriented. Unintended behavior and behavior into which the individual is coerced are outside Sartre's interest. By Sartre's view, the person apprehends a *negatité,* that is, an objective absence of a certain value, entity or situation. The person then wishes to move from the order of the given to the order of the absent being which has been apprehended. Motivation for action does not come from an actual state of affairs but from some possible state of affairs in the future. And it is only against the background of a future possibility that one realizes the present lack. "It is on the day that we can conceive of a different state of affairs that a new light falls on our troubles and our suffering and that we *decide* that these are unbearable." [1]

When we resign ourselves to a distressed situation we do so because we do not experience a *negatité,* or an alternate vision of reality. When an alternate vision is missing, oppressive conditions become "natural" and we accept our lot. But oppressive conditions alone are not sufficient to bring about action. Such conditions must be recognized as unbearable when judged in light of an alternate project. Thus, the factual state of affairs is affirmed or denied by means of the attitude of the individual

[1] Jean-Paul Sartre, *Being and Nothingness,* trans. Hazel E. Barnes (New York: Washington Square Press, 1973), p. 561.

(for-itself). The nihilating power of consciousness along with its capacity to design projects is what allows the given conditions to be judged oppressive. In this connection action is brought about not by past or present events but by the possible events of the future. This position is the central theme of Sartre's theory of action and his existential psychology.

Sartre emphasizes time in his theory of action. In this he is influenced by Heidegger's thesis that human time always temporalizes toward the future. The Self is a temporal being. But time for Sartre is not a fixed or universal scheme of already completed events or of "nows." Time is instead the annihilating movement of the for-itself. The past exists since it was once annihilated by a certain activity of consciousness. It is not a quality inhering in things but a product of human action and consciousness. The past is constituted by my already completed acts. The past is "my consumed possibility." "I can remove nothing [from it] and I can add nothing to it. In other words the past which *I was* is what it is; it is an in-itself like the things in the world." [2]

No matter how factual the reality of the past may be, its *meaning* is contingent on the present. This meaning modifies itself in accordance with one's present engagements. In this sense, the past stands in suspense, that is, it is not an actuality irrevocably fixed. It is something that can always be put into question. It awaits ratification by the free project in the present. The present is given in the project of the person in which the person tries to find stability and permanency. But the attempt to perpetuate the given is futile since the Self is always in "flight from being toward the future." It is only by negating its being that the for-itself comes to recognize itself as given in the present.

In this connection, human motivation cannot be understood to possess a fixed character or nature. Since it is defined by an absent end, it is characterized by the "non-existent." [3] What motivates the organism to act in a certain way is not only the determinant in the present but the freedom of its open future

2 Ibid., p. 170.
3 Ibid., p. 564.

as well. The organism is motivated by a state of "nothingness"—
a state of being yet to be.

Sartre rejects the categorization of parts of the human psyche
into "free" and "unfree." The mind cannot be divided into rational will on the one hand and passion on the other. All acts
manifest the same quality of freedom, since both the will and
the passions are implicated in human action. Both will and passion are the *means* used to carry out a project. Moreover, will
and passion do not precede action. On the contrary, it is the
already completed act which confers meaning upon them. Will
is often equated with a rational type of action, resulting from an
"objective" appraisal of the situation. Passion, on the other hand,
is often equated with the "subjective" attitude of impulsiveness.
We tend to speak of behavior that is preceded by an objective
appraisal as more rational than that which is preceded by a subjective motive. But such a distinction is erroneous, according to
Sartre. There are many instances of the simultaneous operation
of will and passion, cause and motive. These forces are indissoluble, and cannot be divided into certain contrary faculties of
the mind which supposedly determine action. The choice of a
life of bondage or of autonomy and freedom is not determined
by any fact of the psyche but is the result of the future-oriented
project. An external situation does not mechanically cause action.
A situation becomes a cause only when it is comprehended in
light of a project. Even then, the situation becomes merely the
means to carry out the project.

The concept of freedom does not refer to a capricious quality
of mind or to unpredictable acts. A free person simply does not
submit to the customs of the past or to the habits of the present.
It is the free mind which sets its goal, the pursuit of which is
facilitated by what we term "will." And, just as ends and values
may not be determined from without, they likewise cannot be
determined from within, in other words, with reference to an
a priori nature or psyche. It is existence as action which confers
meaning, essence or substance upon reality. And the being of
freedom is existence itself.

Faculties such as will or passion are merely means used to
make connection with the world. They are modalities of existence

which aid the person in developing his project in a certain way. For Sartre, passion or emotion is not a matter of uncontrollable behavior. "It is a reply adapted to [a] situation." [4] Certain situations demand rational and deliberate action while others demand that the emotions be relied upon. Rationality and passions are secondary adaptations to an already formulated project. The project is the fundamental mode by which one has chosen to relate to the world and to express oneself in it. The function of existential psychology is to interpret this fundamental mode, in relation to which every mode of expression, rational or emotional, is secondary.

Thus, radical displays of the emotions are based on the human choice to add, for example, a magical dimension to reality. One person chooses to approach the world by symbolic behavior, another approaches it by rational conduct. It is not the world which determines which of the adaptations should be chosen. The magical and the rational responses do not exist in the world; they are human *means* adapted to a situation in the world.

Cowardliness, inferiority or shamefulness are negative modes of being which manifest themselves after the act. Such modes of being are not a fixed nature of the individual, nor are they imposed upon him from the outside. They are *means* by which the person *chooses* to terminate his freedom, to relieve himself of responsibility, or to give advantage to others.[5] A person chooses a mode of being as the vehicle through which he presents himself to others. It is only as an object, as a being-for-Other that the person appears as passionate, cowardly, capable or weak. Character is, then, constituted through the completed act. It is not a psychic fact or innate datum which exists prior to the act.

Sartre's theory of action relies upon the thesis of *Being and Nothingness* that "being" is illuminated through "nothingness." The non-existent goal orders the values and priorities of the present. Human consciousness exists in the present as a

4 Ibid., p. 574.
5 Ibid., p. 607.

negation of the present. For this reason human choice, denied a foundation in the present, appears to be absurd. It appears to be absurd because it cannot justify itself or excuse itself by the given situation—either past or present. Absurdity lies in human freedom, which searches for itself and annihilates what it finds. For Sartre this does not lead to nihilism, however, but to the autonomy and responsibility of the acting individual.

Existential psychology

Sartre begins the discussion of his existential psychology with the claim that there is no fixed human nature. Consequently, human beings do not conform to "fate" but search for some sort of truth. Existential psychology studies the meaning of this search. It is the study of human *ends*. Sartre's analysis of this topic is neither extensive nor systematic. It is simply an elaboration of his theory of action, a theory which is central to his work in the *Critique*.

Human action is understood by interpreting the ends which are posited for it. Here, the end is not treated as an isolated or random decision but as the product of the person's fundamental choice, that is, the attitude which he takes toward the world. Human behavior reveals itself in many unique and different ways and the task of the existential psychoanalyst is to uncover the meaning of these different types of behavior in relation to the original fundamental choice. The original human choice is given in the individual's life plan, self-image, relationships with others, and so on.

The fundamental choice is not always made enthusiastically. It may be made in a spirit of resignation or helplessness in order to flee from responsibility. For example, the choice of humiliation makes us see ourselves as inferior. Humiliation can appear as our basic attitude toward the world. By means of the mechanism of bad faith, as we noted earlier, the masochistic attitude can relieve us of the anxiety of being responsible actors and can make us into inert and passive being-for-Others. Surrendering to the attitude of being-for-Others, we come to comprehend it as the cause of our situation, while, in fact, it had been our fundamental choice all along. In Sartre's view: "This being-for-Others as a *situation* will act in the capacity of a cause, but all the same it must be discovered by a *motive* which is nothing but our free project. Thus, the inferiority which is felt and lived is the chosen instrument to make us comparable to a *thing*." [6]

Without analysis of the person's fundamental choice, all events connected with his life are meaningless. As to the genesis of fundamental choice, it cannot be reduced to the parameters of conventional psychiatry or sociology, to "desire," "urge," "environment," "economic background" or any other notion. Human choices can have no *cause* or *past,* according to Sartre. Choices are not "consequences" or "functions" of determining forces. The relations which we ordinarily refer to when explaining behavior are notions used to understand cause and effect. We can comprehend them as objective relations and processes while not comprehending a thing about the concrete individual case. We commit the same error by explaining a specific behavior with reference to innate inclinations or predispositions. The "explanatory idols" aim at classifying phenomena rather than at comprehending them. According to Sartre, a person cannot be reconstructed by such "irreducibles." [7] Inferiority, for example, is not a psychic fact that exists with an antecedent whose consequence is an inferior life. No single predisposition or inclination can be isolated from the fundamental choice of the person. He is actually constituted by this original conscious choice as his basic stand toward the world. This choice cannot be understood with analytical definitions and classifications. The fundamental choice possesses a pre-logical status.

Freudian psychologists also attempt to comprehend the fundamental choice. To attain this goal they take the person's total conduct into account. They use the same methods that Sartre himself embraces: diaries, reflection and various other types of information. Sartre, in fact, acknowledges his agreement with the Freudian goal and method. But he challenges the notions

[6] Ibid.
[7] Ibid., p. 718.

used by Freudians to explain their findings, notably those of the "unconscious," the "libido," and the "complex." [8]

Freudian psychoanalysis presupposes the existence of a psyche which precedes the consciousness of the person. Sartre rejects such a view since each and every act is co-existent with consciousness. Every actor consciously makes his choice. What the empirical psychoanalyst sees is merely what *he* "pulls out" of the patient's reflection, which is not the patient's unconscious self but the patient's fundamental choice as seen by the Other. The psychoanalyst merely sees the patient from the point of view of the Other. Thereafter the patient *recognizes* the situation about which he was always really *conscious*. This distinction between recognition and consciousness is Sartre's distinction between knowledge and existence. A person is always conscious of his acts even if he does not always reflect on them. The anxiety experienced by the person during sessions of reflection with the therapist is generated by a new awareness of his responsibility. Therefore, in psychoanalytic sessions the patient does not find a "new" consciousness but a mere reflection of his conscious life. He understands it as a hypothesis which has a high probability of being true because it illuminates a number of his behaviors.

The *unconscious,* for Sartre, is not a hidden substance but a manifestation of *bad faith*. It is a deception on the part of the patient—an act of avoidance. This is why the central principle of existential psychology is "to make every man aware of what he is and to make the full responsibility of his existence rest on him." [9]

In rejecting what he calls fixed antecedents or the irreducibles, Sartre rejects the concept of libido. The concept of libido contradicts the fundamental notion of the person as *freedom* or the *for-itself*. The person aims at appropriating an aspect of the world, or of the in-itself, which is not strictly sexual. There are an infinite number of modes of appropriation and they are

[8] Ibid., pp. 727–34.
[9] Jean-Paul Sartre, *Existentialism and Human Emotions* (New York: The Wisdom Library, 1957), p. 16.

not universal. The libido cannot be universally grasped as a static fact of consciousness. It is nothing save for its manifestation by the particular individual. "There is not first a single desire of being, then a thousand particular feelings, but the desire to be exists and manifests itself only in and through jealousy, greed, love of art, cowardice, courage and a thousand contingent, empirical expressions which always cause human reality to appear to us only as *manifested* by a *particular man,* by a specific person." [10] The manifestations of the libido are manifestations of the unconscious which are *secondary* to the person's fundamental choice, which is conscious.

Moreover, when speaking of an inferiority complex one ought not understand it to refer to an antecedent event which precipitates the course of one's life. The inferiority complex is secondary, and is itself preceded by the person's fundamental choice to exist in an inferior position. It is the product of a life-script of failure, the product of an escape from struggle and power. "This inferiority which I struggle against and which nevertheless I recognize, this I have chosen from the start." [11] Inferiority, inadequacy, ugliness and idiocy are not established in the person as quantitative facts. Instead, they reveal themselves as future-oriented projects. They become manifest as functions of the projects that the actor will choose or of the situation in which he will act.

To sum up the preceding analysis, comprehension of behavior is attained from the point of view of the projects of the individual rather than from his prior fixations. Sartre is not interested in discovering constant givens but in discovering the planned projects of the person. This is the basic difference between Sartre's existential psychology and Freud's psychoanalysis. Freud understands the person in light of antecedents; Sartre understands him in light of his future-oriented projects.

Sartre's rejection of Freudian notions is consistent with his rejection of the idea of essence or substance—or, for that matter, of the idea of God. His rejection is made in defense of the

---

[10] Sartre, *Being and Nothingness,* p. 722.
[11] Ibid., p. 591.

concept of humanity as free and non-determined. Human freedom coincides with *nothingness:* the ground from which human projects come into being without a prior cause or claim. A certain reality comes to man through his action in the world. The meaning of freedom rests in the fact that we can act in the world without prior excuses or causes. This position compels the person to *make himself.* The making of the self entails anguish and anxiety which goes along with the recognition of freedom. Freedom facilitates choice and contains no moral imperative that tells us what to choose. But Sartre adds a qualification to this view. In *Existentialism and Human Emotions* he deals with the moral dilemmas of freedom rather ingeniously. Freedom, he states, carries with it a *collective responsibility* for all men. In choosing, a person chooses for all Others. A person creates himself in the image of what every human being ought to be. "To choose to be this or that is to affirm at the same time the value of what we choose, because we can never choose evil. We always choose the good, and nothing can be good for us without being good for all." In choosing between the religious life or marriage the person involves all of humanity in the choice. He establishes the normative meaning of the resigned life or of the monogamous life as a meaning for all Others. In fact, this is why authentic choice is a source of anguish. For anguish is the awareness that my choice may possess a universal imperative for all other men. And if a person acts without awareness, he is "masking his anguish." [12]

The fact that there may not be a God is distressing, for it means that there is no *a priori* certainty. While this fact makes human beings forlorn, it also heightens the sense of responsibility. One has no excuse; not even the forces of passion can excuse our acts. To opt for good or evil, sanity or madness, is a choice for which we alone are responsible.

The concept of the situation

The notion that men can choose challenges the principle of determinism as found in the sociological concept of the social

[12] Sartre, *Existentialism and Human Emotions*, pp. 16–17, 20.

environment. The social environment reminds the person of his vulnerability, and the arguments in favor of it are the arguments against freedom. By common sense, the person feels "fated," by race, by nationality, by family, or by occupation. His life-long struggle may yield results of little significance. "Much more than he appears to make himself man seems to be made." [13] Nevertheless, the "coefficient of adversity," argues Sartre, is not in things. The social environment, as an ensemble of things, is neutral, and "waits to be illuminated" by a human act or project. A mountain is an obstacle if one desires to build a road through it, but it is an ally if one chooses to view a landscape from it. The mountain itself ought not be comprehended as an objective structure and it is meaningless without human significations. It is my project which constitutes the environment as my adversary or as my helper. And it is the environment, when comprehended by the person in relation to a project, which becomes a *situation*.

A project is not a mere process of mental construction or wishful thinking. It is a state to be realized which is yet to come, and which is distanced from me by my given situation. In fact, it is through my resistance to my given situation that my freedom is given meaning. Freedom and situation appear then as correlates. Given conditions are not an obstacle to freedom but its very basis. "There can be a free for-itself only as engaged in a resisting world. Outside of this engagement the notions of freedom, of determinism, of necessity lose all meaning." [14] Sartre emphasizes that the concreteness of freedom is given *vis-à-vis* our practical projects in a world of materiality. To be free does not mean that one necessarily reaches the chosen objective, only that one can choose. Freedom is not necessarily a correlate of success. Freedom must be an act or at least an attempt to act. A prisoner cannot be said to be free. He is not free to leave the prison at will, but he is free to attempt an escape. Sartre does not distinguish between freedom, choice and acting. Intentions, therefore, are meaningless; they are like

[13] Sartre, *Being and Nothingness,* p. 619.
[14] Ibid., p. 621.

whims or dreams when they are divorced from action. It is the act itself and only the act which makes intentions real for us.

Sartre does not desire to cancel the meaning of one's situation. There is a *residuum* to any situation which is the particular fact of one's social condition. But the given fact is not absolute. It receives its meaning from the human projects inscribed in it. Human ends transform the environment into a particular situation where obstacles and hardships define the projects of freedom itself.

Choice and the ethics of seriousness

For Sartre, choice is a deed which is revealed through every act of consciousness. It is continuously manifest, even through the smallest details of our daily activity, our modes of presenting the self to others, our moods, and so on. Since choice is not external to the acting individual, it does not present itself as an object for reflection and judgment. Judgment itself deals with the accomplished deed. In sum, choice is not a particularly dramatic event; it does not serve as an object of deliberate analysis. This is why it is always subject to change, rejection and replacement.

This view leads to a rejection of the notion that the subjective attitude is constitutive of choice. Choice cannot be defined as such by the wishes, decisions or contemplation of the individual. Instead it constitutes itself as an act which gains its meaning against the background of a concrete situation in the world. Choice and action in a concrete situation are inseparable. The situation is the object of action but without the situation being responsible for it. We saw earlier how the situation by itself cannot cause a choice to come into being. A situation is a neutral given. By itself, it is neither detrimental nor favorable to the person, and whatever qualities it receives are the function of one's ends. One defines the choice from some point in the future. The obstacles which one encounters in a situation are defined to the extent that the situation resists one's project, and it is only in relation to such resistance that one can understand the meaning of freedom.

Human reality caught up in a situation creates a specific ethical problem. Here, the meaning of ethics does not refer to separate acts in relation to which the moral quality of human passion may be put to question, but refers to the person's fundamental choice as a function of his relation to the human world and to materiality. Human beings can relate to material in different manners. A group may choose to give primacy to the environmental forces, and consider them as independent forces which determine its social organization, social values and goals. Or, a group may choose to consider its environment as secondary to its acts and it may employ this very environment as the means to an end. Each of the choices entails incompatible commitments. Each choice will have some effect on the interpretation of freedom, the priorities of life styles, and the social arrangements and values of the group. These rudimentary remarks merely touch upon what becomes a central concern of Sartre in the *Critique,* namely, the mediations of the material world and the effects of this mediation on human groups. The series and praxis groups which will be studied in chapter five are concrete groups which, in their day-to-day existence, embody to a large extent the two types of choice referred to above.

In the last section of *Being and Nothingness* Sartre speculates about the nature of action in the modern world and type of ethics which it represents. He believes that what determines contemporary action (both revolutionary and conservative) is the so-called ethics of seriousness. We already interpreted the spirit of seriousness as the human attitude which grants an irreducible status to the external material and institutional world. In the spirit of seriousness the world appears as independent and as an ultimately determining factor of action. The serious person desires the material world and considers it as a goal and foundation of meaning. In this role, men come to consider themselves as products of the world and to appreciate themselves in terms of their position in such a world. Sartre's description of the ethics of seriousness is penetrating and deserves complete reproduction.

> The serious attitude involves starting from the world and attributing more reality to the world than to oneself; at the

the very least the serious man confers reality on himself to the degree to which he belongs to the world. It is not by chance that materialism is serious; it is not by chance that it is found at all times and places as the favorite doctrine of the revolutionary. This is because revolutionaries are serious. They come to know themselves first in terms of the world which oppresses them, and they wish to change this world. In this one respect they are in agreement with their ancient adversaries, the possessors, who also come to know themselves and appreciate themselves in terms of their position in the world. Thus all serious thought is thickened by the world; it coagulates; it is a dismissal of human reality in favor of the world. The serious man is "of the world" and has no resource in himself. He does not even imagine any longer the possibility of *getting out of* the world, for he has given to himself the type of existence of the rock, the consistency, the inertia, the opacity of being-in-the-midst-of-the-world.[15]

By subordinating himself to the world the serious man wishes to obscure the demands of freedom. It is consciousness (for-itself) escaping anguish by reducing itself to matter (in-itself). The person considers himself as the mere means of an objective state of affairs. His human resources are dismissed in favor of a world in which he adapts through labor. He finds significance outside of himself, in position, possessions and relationship to things.

The quality of the world of things is not a quality of humanity. The quality of such a world is that of a plenitude justified by its own existence. Such a world as the in-itself is fixed, contingent and factual. The primary quality of humanity, on the other hand, is that of "nothingness." It comes from annihilation, negation and transcendence. But contemporary man is tired of transcendence; he desires to bring about a fusion between his projects and his mere existence, and wishes to establish himself in the world of things. Evidently, here the process of "leveling down" is involved. It occurs by way of reduced

15 Ibid., p. 741.

aspirations, and by way of adapting to the technical world. It is a route through which contemporary men put an end to their "higher" aspirations; whereby they renounce the need for new visions and humanization. The ethics of seriousness bring an end to the human struggle with materiality. By uniting objectivity and subjectivity, men will have overcome their alienation along with the state of "unhappy consciousness." Freud, in *Beyond the Pleasure Principle,* also expressed the idea as the desire to regress to the quiescence of the inanimate matter. For Sartre, such an idea is doomed to failure, for to attempt to reconcile humanity and matter is to act in bad faith.

Sartre believes that one's world and one's situation become the responsibility of humanity and not the other way around. Humanity, which deals with its freedom, can appropriate the world not at the command of material necessity but only in pursuit of its human possibilities. A free humanity ruptures the unity of human passion and the material world. A free humanity regains its distance from matter, which distance is the measure of its autonomy. Humanity becomes its own end, in which case the world becomes a human instrument instead of a material fate.

Being, doing and having

The terms "being," "doing" and "having" can be used to summarize what has been analyzed so far. They stand for types of relations which the person assumes toward the world, and for the ethics attendant upon such relations. The terms are neither exclusive nor irreducible.

Being, for Sartre, means to make known what the person *is* as a *possibility.* Being is, therefore, the goal of the for-itself. It is not to be established by empirical or logical proof or argument but is the *a priori* description of the for-itself. Every detail of daily life (e.g., sleeping, thinking, loving or eating) is the same desire *to be,* and expresses the meaning of existence and the for-itself. "The original project of a for-itself can aim only at its being." [16] Similarly, the object of desire is also diversi-

16 Ibid., p. 721.

fied. The object can be food, shelter, another person, but also knowledge, art, religion, and so on. The term *being* is meaningless without action. Being is revealed and defined by a series of chosen acts. Being and doing are therefore not separate.

But the desire to make things may reduce itself to the desire to possess them. One wishes to possess what one creates. Possession embodies the ethics of seriousness and is implicated not only in the economic and material worlds of human life but in the educational, political and scientific worlds as well. In making an object, studying an object, learning about ourselves through an object, and so on, we lessen the distance between man and objects. This occurs because of possessive appropriation and assimilation. Political programs subordinate the individual to the political world. Our knowledge of our selves is derived from an object reality that has been assimilated into humanity. The modern individual discovers and accepts himself as a mere consequence of something other, and he rejoices in the abandoning of himself to the objective sociological or psychological method which regards him as an extension of things, or as a thing itself.

The modern emphasis on objectivity in the social sciences is really an emphasis on the priority of the external world. Objectivity as a method of inquiry abolishes the complexity and the mystery of the for-itself by reducing the individual to the in-itself. The method has its rewards, for it relieves the individual of the tension between inner and outer worlds, but it teaches him to consider his humanity as inferior to the world, thereby taking away his responsibility toward himself and the world alike. The method is used by a 'tired' humanity, whose aim is to become an in-itself and achieve that long desired "indissoluble unity of identity." [17]

But such a synthesis is impossible. The assimilation of things into the self, whether through the appropriation and possession of matter or through the development of knowledge, only produces a feeling of insufficiency and incompleteness in man. The world, both as made and as known, reflects human thought

[17] Ibid., p. 725.

and human subjectivity, but remains outside humanity by maintaining a complete and superior objectivity. It is the world discovered by man which comes to define man as "insufficient" or "incomplete" [18] since sufficiency and completeness rest with objective exteriority.

The impossibility of achieving the total identification between self and matter, of becoming a human-God, produces in man the urge to destroy the made object. The destruction of the made-world is not an infantile act of frustration but is another method of attempting to fuse the object with the self. This negative act of destruction is commensurate with *having*. There is a real enjoyment in the destruction of an object which is very much like the enjoyment produced by appropriation. Destruction, says Sartre, "realizes appropriation perhaps more keenly than creation does, for the object destroyed is no longer there to show itself impenetrable." [19] Destruction is like the "alimentary enjoyment" of possessing. The self incorporates what it destroys for there is a certain sense of consumption involved here.

One of the least possessive aspects of man is found in play. Sartre does not completely deny the appropriative qualities of play. He uses it as a metaphor to point to those ethics which stand in opposition to the spirit of seriousness. For when playing, the person is free. He sets down his own rules. And since playing is not constrained by the material state of objectivity, and because when engaged in it the person is least concerned with possessing another being in the world, it points to what is most essentially human.

Death and the spirit of seriousness

It is worthwhile to compare Sartre's ideas on death with those of Norman O. Brown. Such a contrast should prove to be relevant, since Sartre failed to emphasize the importance of the human attitude toward death and the possible effect of this attitude on ethics and human action.

[18] Ibid., p. 755.
[19] Ibid., p. 757.

Unlike other existentialists who deal seriously with the problem of death, Sartre almost dismisses it. According to Sartre, death neither adds to nor detracts from life. The only thing which it shares with life is *absurdity*. For Heidegger death is inseparable from life. For to die is an integral aspect of life, an open possibility. Heidegger even speaks of "being-for-death," and "being-toward-death," an open end toward which existence is projected. The fact that the person exists along with the possibility of dying is partly responsible for human dread. According to Heidegger, death is a highly personalized event, a subjective possibility which "nobody [else] can undergo for me." In his view, most authentic existential attitudes come from the anticipation of one's own death.[20]

Most of Sartre's analysis of death is a rebuttal of Heidegger's work on the topic. Sartre maintains that death possesses no unique position over any other aspect of the human being. According to Sartre, it is not only *my death* that the Other fails to "undergo"; the Other cannot undergo for me as well my experiences of love, anger, hope, freedom.

According to Sartre, death is a boundary and a limit to one's possibilities. It forever remains outside of one's possibilities. Not being a project, death cannot affect the meaning of life or of my freedom. Hence, death is denied both a future and an intrinsic meaning.[21]

In a sense, one's death is the property of the Other since he is at liberty to take toward it whatever attitudes he wishes. He may wish to reconstruct that life through memories or monuments, or may wish to remain indifferent to it. According to Sartre, "[t]o be dead is to be a prey for the living. This means therefore that the one who tries to grasp the meaning of his future death must discover himself as the future prey of others." [22] The deceased becomes a recipient of objective meanings conferred upon him which he cannot escape. Sartre implies that to

[20] Martin Heidegger, *Being and Time,* trans. John Macquarrie and Edward Robinson (New York: Harper and Row, 1962), pp. 279–311.
[21] Sartre, *Being and Nothingness,* p. 691.
[22] Ibid., p. 695.

be dead for the Other is not the same as being-for-Other, since one is denied the power to annihilate the Other or to transcend him as a for-itself. Sartre therefore concludes that to be dead is simply a contingent fact, one aspect of being-in-situation which has the same weight as one's past, one's environment or one's fellow men, and this does not affect the freedom of the self.

One social theory which remains concerned about human death, finitude and separation is propounded by Norman O. Brown in *Life Against Death*. Brown contends that our organic fate and the attitude we take toward this fate shape the meaning of life itself. For Brown, death is neither an individual matter nor an objective phenomenon but a clue which explains socio-historical forces. It can be used to explain the historical commitment to the building of empires, the conquest of nations, the rise of religion and culture and all those activities that confer continuity and immortality upon men. Historical reason lends support to humanity in its struggle against the absurd interruption of life by death. Man creates the idea of history in order to overcome the anxiety of death. In economic activity, rituals surrounding death, and the concept of resurrection itself, one notices the human desire to flee from the facticity of death. History-making is an attempt to repress the anxiety of human finitude. To understand the human malaise in general one should investigate humanity's relation to death, Brown says:

> It is not the consciousness but the Unconscious flight from death that distinguishes men from animals. From the times of the earliest cave men, who kept their dead alive by dyeing the bones red and burying them near the family hearth, down to the Hollywood funeral cult, the flight from death has been ... the heart of all religion. Pyramids and sky scrapers—monuments more lasting than bronze—suggest how much of the world's "economic" activity also is really a flight from death.[23]

[23] Norman O. Brown, *Life Against Death: The Psychoanalytical Meaning of History* (Middletown, Conn.: Wesleyan University Press, 1959), p. 100.

It is upon the onset of sublimation that the historical person renounces his body and instrumentalizes it as means. He wants to be other than he is, and arrives at this otherness by repressing his bodily drives and desires. Repression, as sublimation, creates a distance between self and body; repression ends the desire for immediate gratification and educates the individual to postpone fulfillment. But to repress one's body is to negate reality, which is what the historical ego is educated to do. The historical ego creates itself by denying its natural condition. This denial requires an involvement in the worlds of religion, economy, politics, science and ideology. But no matter how lasting the achievements may be in these worlds, they remain alien to humanity's authentic needs since they constitute a joyless transformation of the primary and most immediate satisfactions of life. Through sublimation, the human being becomes serious, a creature of toil and renunciation, an instrument of historical reason and action.

Brown's analysis and conclusions are evidently influenced by Freud. And while his views have little in common with Sartre, the implications of these views are close to Sartre's position on the ethics of seriousness. For Brown, historical action results from the fear of death. In the context of historical action the individual's worth is given in relation to an abstract group project. He regards himself as secondary to the world, and accepts the instrumental ethos of history along with the spirit of seriousness. In this connection, Sartre maintains that the individual "makes himself such that he is *waited for* by all the tasks placed along his way. Objects are mute demands, and he is nothing in himself but the passive obedience to these demands." [24]

Although there are many things on which Sartre and Brown do not concur, they both seem to believe that such an ethos dominates the world today. It appears in the form of a positivistic mentality, a primacy of materiality over the human spirit, a reliance upon standard techniques to solve problems, a set of "objective" methods used to study ourselves, and a tacit agree-

[24] Sartre, *Being and Nothingness,* p. 796.

ment to regard the "soft" human desires as useless and inferior. This ethos is common to all members of contemporary society, regardless of class or life style.[25] Our daily conduct rests on an ensemble of materiality and attendant techniques of control and organization. This world extends beyond the particular world-views of any given type of contemporary political culture.

Shrewdness, necessity, constraint and struggle appeal to our serious sense of life. Serious humanity transforms life into a burden and must be, therefore, rigid and uncompromising. Neitzsche expresses the thought aptly in referring to this very spirit. "I found again my old devil and arch-enemy, the *spirit of gravity,* and all it created: constraint, statute, necessity and consequence and purpose and will and good and evil."[26]

It was humanity which created such a world, only to separate itself from it and regard it as an objective value. Economic realities, the necessity of labor, of politics, of science, and so on, become facts of life or the objective order of the world. This is the concept of objectification or human praxis becoming objectivity, an idea which Sartre follows up in the *Critique* in the most concrete terms.

I may have crossed the line of propriety by shifting from analysis to ethics. But this was inescapable. The last pages of *Being and Nothingness* constitute the ethical implications of that work. Sartre says that we cannot derive imperatives from indicatives, or values from descriptions. But by describing states of human consciousness we can arrive at the origin of meaning. The theory of action reveals to the person the fact that he is the *being by whom values exist.* This knowledge makes freedom self-conscious. And the result of self-conscious freedom is social responsibility.

[25] Gila Hayim, "Modern Reality Strategies: An Analysis of Weber, Freud and Ellul," *Human Studies* 1 (1978): 245–59.

[26] Friedrich Nietzsche, *Thus Spoke Zarathustra,* in *The Portable Nietzsche,* ed. Walter Kaufmann (New York: The Viking Press, 1968), p. 309.

four

Materiality

and

sociality

Introduction to the *Critique*

The Critique of Dialectical Reason is a remarkable phenomenological analysis of the human group. In it, Sartre portrays with compassion aspects of human hope and accomplishment, as well as aspects of passivity and fear. Except for the first sections, the analysis is concrete and deals with the human struggle in a world of both material and spiritual forces.

Contrary to some thinkers who portray the *Critique* as radically different from *Being and Nothingness,* I find a real connection between the two.[1] The basic concepts in *Being and Nothingness* prove indispensable for the understanding of the *Critique.* These concepts, in fact, anticipate the thematic concerns which appear in the later work. In *Being and Nothingness* the person was identified by Sartre as an organism which lacks. In the *Critique,* the concept of lack appears again as the state of *being-in-need.* In both works the lack is not only a subjectively cognitive-affective state of being but one in which the individual objectively faces the world, a world of materiality and of Others. Lack or being-in-need imposes common problems and motivates group life. Within it the individual enters

[1] A summary of the controversy appears in the introduction to James F. Sheridan, Jr., *Sartre: The Radical Conversion* (Athens, Ohio: Ohio University Press, 1969).

into agreements with others to produce various forms of affiliations, ideology and action. The emergent human group contains relations of both reciprocity and conflict, of solidarity and deflection, and Sartre's treatment of these phenomena occupies the larger part of the *Critique*.

Confrontation with the material world makes annihilation a permanent possibility for the human organism. To protect itself against that threat, the organism must work with matter. But to act upon the environment a part of the person must return to the level of *inertia*. The person becomes an instrument, a tool, and *recognizes* himself as such. This is created by the relation of labor as the bond between the individual and the group. The material world, as worked by humanity, becomes another object for analysis in the *Critique*. Materiality, as an aspect of nature and as an aspect of the social world, constitutes the primary bond between the organism and the environment, and emerges as a central point of analysis in the *Critique*. But in Sartre's unique comprehension of materiality, he always posits matter in conjunction with human praxis. The relation between matter and praxis is the relation between the in-itself and the for-itself, both of which serve as central concepts in *Being and Nothingness*.

In abstracting the sociological themes of the *Critique* I make few references to traditional or mainstream sociology. My references to Max Weber and George H. Mead in the preceding chapters were necessary in so far as I had to translate the philosophical concerns of *Being and Nothingness* into concerns of daily social life, and to elucidate some of its more "opaque" concepts by allusion to familiar knowledge. I thereby hope to have made *Being and Nothingness* more understandable for the reader in the social sciences.

In dealing with the *Critique*, there is no need to resort to such a method since the text is unique in terms of method, conceptualization and language, and because it deals directly with the concrete experience of sociality, that is, with topics closer to the mind of the social scientist than the themes in *Being and Nothingness*.

Interpretations based on texts external to the *Critique* would be appropriate if one plans to reveal its political and social origins, for example, or those philosophical ideas which influence the author. There is no doubt that such interpretations are legitimate since some sections of the *Critique* are influenced by Descartes, Hegel, Husserl and others. This, however, is not the objective of a sociological, exegetical study of the *Critique*. Nevertheless, one should not, for example, ignore Sartre's recurrent mention of Marx and Engels, especially in the first sections of the *Critique*. In that section one senses Sartre's ambivalence with what he calls dogmatic Marxism, along with his indignation with the thought of Engels.

Sartre, Marx and the Marxists

Sartre claims that the natural scientific emphasis on independent material structures produced a type of Marxist methodology of history that is basically a methodology of exteriority since it considers "the Nature of man [as lying] outside him in an *a priori* law, in an extra human nature, in a history that begins with the nebulae." Such methodology diminishes the human component in history, and human history therefore becomes a branch of natural history. Sartre concludes that this sort of position sides not with humans but with things. The heart of this criticism is directed at Engels' theory of nature. Sartre cites a particularly crude statement by Engels, that "[t]he materialist outlook on nature means nothing more than the conception of nature just as it is, without alien addition." [2] Here, the "alien addition" is apparently the human individual, who by this manner of thinking is expelled from the world. Sartre adds that the laws which Engels supposedly discovered in Nature— the laws of quality/quantity of transformation, of opposites and of negation—are laws which Engels himself put into nature. They are, ironically, three laws which were developed by Hegel as the laws of *thought*.

This is not to say that references to authentic Marxism are

[2] Jean-Paul Sartre, *Critique of Dialectical Reason,* trans. Alan Sheridan-Smith, ed. Jonathan Ree (London: NLB, 1976), p. 27.

absent in Sartre's work. But when they appear they are characterized by a spirit of argumentation and reprimand instead of identification. Grene's observation on this point seems to be appropriate. "In all his professions of faith, and despite the care with which he expounds or takes issue with some classical Marxist texts (notably with Engels) in the *Critique* itself. Sartre's 'Marxism' appears as somehow strained and artificial." [3] His well-known declaration in *Search for a Method,* that Marxism is the victorious philosophy of the twentieth century (of which existentialism is an auxiliary discipline) does not contradict this impression. Over and over again he speaks of Marxist thought as *regulative ideas* capable of multiple interpretations, and he resists all shades of dogmatism. He writes: "The contemporary Marxist finds [such ideas] clear, precise, and unequivocal; for him they *already* contribute a knowledge. We think, on the other hand, that everything remains to be done; we must find the method and constitute the science." [4]

Sartre credits Marx for having rejected the idealistic rules of history whereby history is understood through a philosophical system of knowledge. He also credits Marx for having established the connection between material life and the life of knowledge.[5]

According to Sartre, dialectical reason stands in stark contrast to analytical reason. Analytical reason regards the human mind as an independent entity which freely shapes the world, while remaining free from the consequences of its action. In contrast, dialectical reason (introduced into modern philosophy by Hegel) deals with the inter-relations between mind and the world of action. What man materializes in the world leads to his own alienation from the products of his action. This is the situation of divided consciousness, according to Hegel, where "consciousness of life, of its existence and action, is merely pain

[3] Marjorie Grene, *Sartre* (New York: New View Points, 1973), pp. 186–87.

[4] Jean-Paul Sartre, *Search for A Method,* trans. Hazel E. Barnes (New York: Vintage Books, 1968), p. 35.

[5] Ibid., p. 23.

and sorrow over this existence and activity." [6] But this state of unhappy divided consciousness can be overcome, in Hegel's view, with the aid of knowledge and with the help of philosophy.

Marx adopted the dialectical view but rejected Hegel's conclusions. According to Marx, Hegel dealt with the phenomenon of alienation as though it were a mere state of mind. But Marx viewed the very same phenomenon as the result of inhuman relations of production which had to be surpassed not only philosophically but concretely as well. Human suffering is not only a philosophical problem but an historical fact. Sartre agrees with Marx that history is not a mere idea but a dialectical process—that is, a process by which a person makes his world, and in turn, it is a process by which he is made by the world.[7] The notion of "dialectic" stands, then, for a relationship between the person and the constituted object (i.e., his world).

For Sartre, humanity and world are not totalities but movements or acts of totalization "in the making," initiated by human praxis. It is the person, therefore, who is responsible for his world. Sartre emphasizes the *human project* in its relation to the world. With this emphasis he means to develop an idea of humanity which is not mechanistic or positivistic, or which conforms to the orthodox tenets of dogmatic Marxism. Sartre contends that the real meaning of dialectic has been obscured by modern Marxists. Through "bureaucratic conservatism," present day Marxism views history as a frozen entity. Dogmatic Marxists have, by Sartre's view, eliminated the humanistic component of Marx's original idea. They have had a recourse to *a priori* schemata, schemata which treat universal and objective processes as separate from human praxis. History, for these dogmatists, is classified, universalized—a finished story.[8]

[6] G. W. F. Hegel, *The Phenomenology of Mind,* trans. with an introduction and notes by J. B. Baille (New York: Humanities Press, 1949), second edition, p. 252.

[7] Sartre, *Search for A Method,* pp. 13–14.

[8] Ibid., pp. 29, 53.

Sartre also condemns what he refers to as "lazy Marxism." Lazy Marxism leads to the sort of criticism of historical events which is not derived from experience or the study of particular historical acts, but which relies on inherited categories which are general (for example, category of "class," or "relations of production"). In this way Sartre defends Valéry's work which the Marxists had criticized as being idealistic and bourgeois. By subsuming the real person under pre-constituted and general types, each event in one's life comes to be seen as an inevitable outcome of general historical conditions. In this way other specific factors which require study, such as the family and group relations, are swept away. By situating every work of art, every event, every epoch within a universal historical continuum, Marxists cease to learn anything new. When this is done, "Marxism situates [events] but no longer discovers anything." [9]

"Basis" and "superstructure" are undoubtedly co-constituted. The relation between them is, however, mediated by the individual, according to Sartre. Life is not merely economic in character, and any such vulgar reduction is simply dogmatism.[10]

The person operates on several levels, including the "level" of individual life. Sartre reproaches Engels in particular, who, like many Marxists since, viewed the given economic conditions of a society as a force which alone precipitates the movement of history. Economic conditions exist and influence behavior but they are not forces independent of human praxis. They are the work of men, and their objectivity is constituted by facts of human objectification. They can always be surpassed.[11] If material forces appear to be objective or alien to men, it is because they have not yet learned to identify the human acts which constitute them. Upon gaining such comprehension, in Sartre's view, we eliminate mystification and increase our sense of responsibility. In fact, this type of comprehension is promised in the *Critique*.

Sartre also criticizes structural analysis in American social

[9] Ibid., p. 57.
[10] Ibid., p. 66.
[11] Ibid., p. 87.

science. The work of Kurt Lewin, for example, though Lewin is not a Marxist, shares with dogmatic Marxism the same error of general categorization. Both orthodox Marxism and structuralism of Lewin's sort view reality as something that is preconstituted rather than as a process open and variant.[12] For Lewin, each law is a structural phenomenon which relates function to system as "part" to "whole." Lewin, then, can be criticized for elevating individual acts to the level of general, non-individual phenomena.

Social life is affected by certain trans-personal processes, but it is also affected by its human goals in the future. The fact that human action is oriented toward a goal makes each human enterprise a *project*. And a human project is "a flight and leap ahead, at once a refusal and a realization." The theme of refusal for Sartre is one of negation. It is a central concept in *Being and Nothingness* and stands in opposition to mechanistic determinism with which "Marxists allow themselves to be duped." [13]

There have been attempts to eliminate conflict between existentialism and Marxism by merging the two philosophical positions. Poster provides a definition for this sort of merger. According to him, such a merger has to take into account advanced industrial society with all its attendant everyday relations and not only the relations of production. Such a social philosophy would articulate the praxes responsible for creating the human world and it would reject the notion of a closed and already completed theory.[14] Such a merger appears to be theoretical, however, since Sartre himself claims that the work of Marx "lacks any hierarchy of mediation which would permit it to grasp the process which produces the person and his product inside a class within a given society at a given historical moment." [15]

[12] Ibid., p. 69.
[13] Ibid., pp. 92, 96.
[14] Mark Poster, *Existential Marxism in Postwar France: From Sartre to Althusser* (Princeton: Princeton University Press, 1975), p. ix.
[15] Sartre, *Search for A Method,* p. 56.

The method

A basic difference between Sartre's treatment of sociality in the *Critique* and its treatment by mainstream sociologists (including all structural and Marxist work) is the fact that Sartre begins with the person, instead of with institutional structures. He follows up the practical relations of the individual, involving his various contradictions, struggles with others and so on, until the individual "fuses" with a group, an institution, or simply becomes a social/historical personality. Sartre admits that the person is an incomplete abstraction before he has been constituted by his social determinations. But beginning with such an abstract and incomplete identity does not atomize the project of the *Critique,* since an individual act is always a cultural act.

The theoretical transition from individual action to multiplicity (Sartre's term for a human collective) does not mean that the collective reality is reduced to the individual actor. The two methods, of either reducing the individual to the institution or reducing the institution to the individual, do not work for Sartre. He focuses on the active and practical transformations which occur as humanity acts upon itself and upon matter. It is the study of the human group in its various stages of social transformation, with the aim of producing intelligibility. Intelligibility is the quest for comprehension which is the heart of the *Critique.*

Sartre's concern with intelligibility carries significance for the sociological enterprise. The language of mainstream sociology is basically a language of things and of institutions, not of persons, which is why it generates a sense of artificiality and massification. Sartre creates a different language, which is significant because it can understand and interpret active points of historical transition as well as changes in states of being in the social daily experience. Complex sociological concepts such as class, bureaucracy, role, collective, group, and so forth, are analyzed by Sartre *in vivo,* which produces a powerful sense of empathy in the reader. The reader recognizes, in himself and others, the constant movement between freedom and submission, between the exhilarating feeling in the intended act and the entanglements of its unintended consequences. The abstract and the concrete (as exemplified in the actor and in his social products) engage in a "methodological reciprocity."

Human action cannot be free and intended all the time since it is inextricably bound to materiality and necessity. Necessity is the property of worked matter which is dialectically related to the active person. It becomes a requirement in all human projects, and therefore emerges as a cardinal point in the *Critique*. Sartre's analysis of necessity is not alien to his system. In *Being and Nothingness,* where one finds the concepts of the *en-soi,* the Other and the situation, Sartre already dealt with necessity and pointed out its relation to the notion of freedom. The relationship between the for-itself and the in-itself, or between consciousness and its environing field, points not only to relations between the conscious individual and inert matter, but also to the fact that the inorganic is interiorized, ". . . quantity produces in each member of a group a thick layer of inertia (exteriority within interiority). . . ." [16] The idea of necessity is not a new orientation in Sartre, and is not what some call the "radical conversion" from *Being and Nothingness* to the *Critique,* whereby Sartre supposedly rejects the free individual.[17]

Sartre notes that when he speaks of the organism in need, he is not speaking of isolation as an existential state, but of isolation imposed by certain modes of division of labor or social arrangements. Contrary to common belief, the concept of isolation is really foreign to Sartre's line of thinking, as evidenced from this typical quote: "It is impossible to *exist amongst men* without their becoming objects both for me and for them through me, without my being an object for them, and without my subjectivity getting its objective reality through them. . . ." [18] This view of intersubjectivity has already appeared in *Being and Nothingness.* Sartre also rejects the possibility of isolation on perceptual and phenomenological grounds. He maintains

[16] Sartre, *Critique,* p. 72.

[17] See Mary Warnock, *The Philosophy of Sartre* (Hutchinson University Library, 1965).

[18] Sartre, *Critique,* p. 105.

that the mere perceiving of any isolated phenomenon creates a relationship for me and thereby constitutes me. There is a phenomenological reciprocity which operates at the elementary structure of perception itself.

In addition to the perceptual bond between individuals, they are also mediated *vis-à-vis* one another through tools, instruments and institutions. But, and most importantly, individuals are bound to each other by means of their orientation toward the future. This future orientation comes from their shared desire to recreate or change the world. While the implication of these statements may mean that we are related to each other in a common cause, such relatedness can also be one of conflict. Relations of conflict are not, however, a function of our search for recognition, as Hegel contended, but a function of materiality. As instruments of labor we are reduced to materiality, since this is the only way we can act upon matter. Consequently our material environment absorbs a great deal of our human powers and becomes laden with human values. It is this inert material ensemble, now significantly saturated with human properties, which leads to conflict. In conflict ". . . every one reduces himself to his materiality so as to act on that of the Other; through pretences, stratagems, frauds and manoeuvers every one allows himself to be constituted by the Other as a *false object, a deceptive means.*" [19]

When Sartre treats matter, he does not refer to the pure matter which constitutes nature, but to that matter which is significant from the perspective of human labor. Matter by itself cannot produce a relation between men. It becomes relevant only after having received its "seal of unity" from human projects. It is this type of worked matter which is the pre-condition for human history. Matter is unified by means of human acts and does not possess an inherent force independent of men's projects. Gold by itself is pure materiality, a passive substance whose meaning comes to it through man. This relation between matter and men may be understood with the concept of scarcity.

For Sartre, the idea of scarcity is based on worked matter.

[19] Ibid., p. 113.

Gold becomes *scarce* only after having become significant *vis-à-vis* human projects. Scarcity in this context is *produced*, it is a value "transmitted to matter through men and returning to men through matter." [20]

The fact that scarcity is a basic human relation to nature is not denied by Sartre. However, he feels that beyond a primary dependence on nature, additional and new forms of scarcity have been unnecessarily produced. Furthermore, one cannot say, by Sartre's view, that one has discovered in material scarcity the sole force behind history. Scarcity alone, as an objective material force, does not initiate the historical and cultural process. For example, there are backward societies whose members were subject to impoverished environmental circumstances and who experienced a long-standing scarcity without producing a history. The forms of technology and social organization do not necessarily develop as a result of scarcity, though they are produced in a "milieu of scarcity." Scarcity can serve as the basis for a particular type of human history, such as ours, whereby the individual interiorizes scarcity as the ultimate structure of his relations to the world and to Others. [21] Scarcity by itself is not sufficient to bring about an historical cultural reality.

In a milieu which is accepted as that of scarcity everyone becomes a threat to the Other. Each person understands that every other person is a consumer of something he himself needs. This is where social conflict is introduced. The individual, under these circumstances, exists as a mere "thing," an objective fact, an Other, to be manipulated or even annihilated in the name of scarcity. This non-human element which is initiated in all of us is basically the result of having interiorized materiality. The recognition that the Other is a threat, materially, promotes a network of relations based on fear and violence. Such relations constitute the ethics of scarcity as a *chosen relationship* between humanity and its environment. Sartre describes the effects of this ethic as follows: "Nothing—not even wild beasts or microbes—could be more terrifying for man than a species

20 Ibid., p. 123.
21 Ibid., p. 127.

which is intelligent, carnivorous and cruel, and which can understand and outwit human intelligence, and whose aim is precisely the destruction of man. This, however, is obviously our own species as perceived in others by each of its members in the context of scarcity." [22]

A material field is defined by Sartre not only by a collection of commodities but by its human constituents as well. This happens when the Other is viewed as a threat, in the context of scarcity, or when the Other is recognized as an *object* to be destroyed or exploited. In this context the Other is seen as identical to all other objects in the material field.

So far this has been the typical historical experience of human beings. Throughout history, the transformation of the inert world into a human world (totalization) has been achieved by using matter as the object of human praxis. Matter is the so-called inverted praxis, which reflects human labor. Praxis instrumentalizes matter and the material environment and confers organic unity upon them. Matter is thus totalized; it gains its own idea, begins to live in communion with the laborer and becomes inseparable from human sociality.

Hegel, Marx and others showed how matter can differentiate institutions, relations of production, systems of property, and thereby generates struggle. But in addition to their notions of struggle (man against nature and against other men) Sartre introduces another order of struggle in which the individual has to struggle against the products of his own praxis. By Sartre's view, action is not solely determined by the original need, but by the effects of one's own satisfactions (products). This is the idea of the practico-inert, as anti-praxis, which is basic to the *Critique* and which will be followed up later. It denotes the fact that since the product falls outside of the control of the actor, it becomes filled with its own power and status and thereby imposes limitations on future forms and types of action. Thus the transformation of nature by human labor can have its own anti-human consequences. What begins originally as a conscious act can bring about rigid and unin-

22 Ibid., pp. 130, 132.

tended results which condition and limit the freedom of future praxis. Matter, which absorbs human labor, produces its own results regardless of intention.

In our dealing with matter we experience an element of necessity with respect to the anticipated results. These results are not contingent on a subjective attitude but are there, in fact, to the extent that our praxis and the tools we use are rational and deliberate. It is like when we go about a mathematical operation. The result achieved at the other end of the equation is always a *necessary* but a radical result not always prefigured by the agent. The results are partially the product of objective method and objective conditions and are not solely to be traced to the agent. This accounts for our experience of the inevitable character of the practico-inert. "The experience of necessity is all the more obvious, all the more blinding, to the extent that every moment of the *praxis* has been clear and conscious, and that the choice of means has been deliberate. And it should be remembered that, as it becomes richer, *praxis* gradually reduces the number of possibilities to one and, in the end, eliminates itself . . . in favor of a result inscribed in things." [23] The implications of such a position are radical, for the consequences of human praxis which contribute to the building up of the practico-inert will side with the method of materiality, thus diminishing human choice and freedom. This conclusion is remarkably similar to Ellul's work in *Technological Society*. Because of technique and the practico-inert, the human agent diminishes through his products, and begins to trail behind what he objectifies through his praxis. The results of his action become other than what he himself intends and desires. Hence, necessity appears not as an exterior force, as something that opposes praxis, but is the *objective* result of the free praxis of the human actor. And, ironically, it is precisely when we are most rational and responsible that we discover such necessity as ineluctible. The practico-inert is our freedom exteriorized. In this context, the practico-inert generates a forceful experience of alienation, which is not the Marxist conception of alien-

23 Ibid., p. 226.

ation, founded on exploitation, but the Hegelian concept of alienation in which the labor of the person returns to him in the form of "another."

This is the fatal character of all praxes, where one is objectified in something outside of oneself (for example, in matter, which is not one's own) thereby discovering oneself as "another" in the totalized object.[24]

Praxis and practico-inert are bound to one another and form the dialectics of the *pour-soi* and the *en-soi,* of consciousness and matter, of objectification which becomes objectivity. These different relations account for what humanity does with its freedom in the various stages of its encounter with materiality; or, in the style of Sartre, they account for the manner in which humanity totalizes its destiny.

The concepts of praxis, practico-inert and necessity, which serve as basic concepts in the *Critique,* are, in my view, social representations of the concepts in *Being and Nothingness.* Praxis embodies the intending consciousness as a free agent, that is, as the for-itself. This human attribute always desires to appropriate the world, since desire is characteristic of a lack. The object of human fulfillment lies outside the actor, in the exteriority of matter, and serves as the foundation for historical action. Human consciousness, as a structure of freedom, delegates its power to the inert environment and creates its human products. The totalized environment becomes worked matter which reflects back the massification of disparate individual actions. Totalized matter, the in-itself or *en-soi,* is the concretized world of the actor. The actor recognizes and defines himself through totalized matter (as in identifying with one's tools, products, institutions and so on). In this connection totalized matter is "... [the] vampire object [which] constantly absorbs human action, lives on blood taken from man and finally lives in symbiosis with him." [25] One realizes that free praxis stands on the side of a totalizing humanity and that necessity stands on the side of the finished product or the practico-inert.

24 Ibid., p. 227.
25 Ibid., p. 169.

These statements bring the analysis of the *pour-soi* in *Being and Nothingness* to its historical conclusion. The person, as pure *pour-soi,* is meaningless, abstract and incomplete until he has anchored himself in the world as an historical being. This does not counteract the person's freedom, however, since Sartre's concept of praxis stands for the negation of every particular given and for its higher reorganization for future acts of satisfaction.

Sartre wishes to introduce a new dialectic in the study of social reality. It is a dialectic which gives primacy to the human factor over the world of matter. Sartre acknowledges the circular movement between man and the forces of his environment. But in his view, there is no predetermined direction to this movement. Humanity is not a passive wheel but makes itself, and in the process of making itself it *surpasses* the given. Sartre's *Critique* is a *critique* of the method which views and treats humanity and world as static entities (totalities) whose interconnections follow a predetermined path, in the spirit of the dogmatic version of dialectical reason.

five

The human group:

serial and

praxis groups

Serial group: the sociology of human inertia

                     An extreme case of intersubjectivity, based on the mediation of objects and inertia, is what Sartre calls the *serial collective*. The serial collective is a human group which is defined solely by a common product or object situated outside it. The common object (for example, a bus stop, a red light, a building or a bread line) defines this plurality of persons as *serial*. It is not difficult to imagine an object serving as the organizational center for otherwise unrelated persons. This phenomenon is typical of everyday life, in the neighborhood, at work, in places of entertainment and so on. In fact, it is a most rudimentary form of sociality in which self-definition and a sense of purpose are completely determined by one's position among objects and in relation to objects. (Sartre himself gives the example of individuals waiting for a bus, at a bus stop, as a simple illustration of such a group.)

Seriality is common to all unorganized and marginal human groups. It stands for feelings of isolation, powerlessness and alienation. The analysis of seriality is, therefore, the sociology of human inertia. It arises from a concentration of collective objects, a technical milieu and an atomized society. Seriality denotes the decomposition of communal relations, and the enhancement of relationships between persons and things.

If we return to the example of the bus queue, we find that

a certain type of relationship exists between all waiting persons, which is essentially a non-relationship of isolation. The members of such a group are devoid of care or concern for one another. They merely exist serially, that is, side by side. "This man is isolated not only by his body as such, but also by the fact that he turns his back on his neighbor who, moreover, has not even noticed him (or has encountered him in his practical field as a general individual defined by waiting for the bus)." [1] Every person in such a group is defined by the simple fact that he is waiting for the bus. But Sartre remarks that no matter how acute a sense of isolation may be, it nevertheless presupposes reciprocity. He nearly paraphrases Durkheim when he states that isolation cannot free the person from the impact of the Other, since we all submit to conventions, habits, manners and other rules of various sorts which are not the property of any one person.

The members of the serial group are united by a similar interest which is imposed from the outside, from the domain of the practico-inert—a bus service. Such a group possesses some type of cohesion, but this cohesion is produced by a ticket machine or some other common object or artifact outside of the group. The external object not only dictates the seriality of the members of the group but also renders the members interchangeable. Members of a serial group are interchangeable because they are not socially differentiated. The only basis for their differentiation is their organic identity. The absence of differentiation occurs when internal qualities of the members are negated, and when the members are joined as mere *Others*. "Everyone is the same as the Others in so far as he is Other than himself." [2] Their unity is passive. A collective is constituted by virtue of the fact that each member exists outside of himself as a part of a plurality. Everyone's identity lies in an all-consuming exteriority where Otherness is the only social determinator.

[1] Jean-Paul Sartre, *Critique of Dialectical Reason,* trans. Alan Sheridan-Smith, ed. Jonathan Ree (London: NLB, 1976), p. 256.
[2] Ibid., p. 260.

In a generic sense, seriality ought to be regarded as the product of the practico-inert. Whenever the practico-inert dominates our material environment (for example, mechanized tools, complex institutions, automated devices and so on), a seriality of human relationships based on things is plausible. Relationships become defined and coordinated by the forces of inertia and the forms of exteriority. In those social structures more complex than the "bus group," seriality is more highly differentiated. Under certain social conditions seriality is not contingent, for example, upon the visual presence of all members, in other words, it does not have to be direct. Serial relationships can exist indirectly (as in listening to the same program, watching the same show, sharing the same problem and so on). Furthermore, when one or all members (listeners, watchers) of such a group experience indignation at the content of the program, they also experience powerlessness. This powerlessness comes from an absence of mutual essentiality and from a passive sense of group membership. The power of the practico-inert field is enhanced in proportion to this sense of powerlessness. No individual action (for example, the turning off of the T.V. in protest) can effect the slightest change in the actual broadcasting. With such an act, "I will not have negated the voice; I will have negated myself as an individual member of the gathering." [3]

The notion of a serial being is radical in so far as the sociality of this being is not defined by tradition, moral obligation, a certain world-view or any other general sociological concept. It is defined instead by the structure of a tool or an object outside it. In this sense serial being becomes an aspect of the passive practico-inert. Serial gatherings are thus the most elementary structures of sociality since they reflect the general thesis of Sartre that simple sociality is fundamentally produced by things—that sociality rests on a bond with materiality.

On the more complicated level of association, in a factory, for example, all appearances of solidarity (between workers, managers, employers and so on) are also based on seriality.

[3] Ibid., p. 272.

The concerted activity of production which takes into account all levels of skill is made possible by an object—in the form of a product—which confers on the workers a serial unity. "... [A]nd if it can make people believe in the existence of an original agreement where there is, in fact, only an anti-social (practico-inert) force, this is because its passive unity, in its radical heterogeneity, cannot refer to any kind of human unification." Worked materiality—a product carrying anonymous praxis—is the center of serial unity in the factory. A common object organizes the members of this group and defines them as designers, laborers, owners and so on. The inhuman effects of this aspect of the practico-inert are particularly apparent when the product becomes an autonomous commodity, when it becomes not a function of real needs but an "independent" object. The common independent object almost becomes a destiny. Its inflexibility (as expressed for example in the laws of economy, the forms of bureaucracy and so on) increases the sense of powerlessness of members of the group, thereby, according to Sartre, free praxis becomes emptied of meaning.[4]

The practico-inert, as the center of the serial activity, constitutes a limiting world, a world in which *praxis* has been converted into *exis*. In this context, the practico-inert assumes co-existence with its own producer, in the form of commodities, technical environment, exigencies, institutions, artifacts, tools and so on. "I need only glance out of the window: I will be able to see cars which are men and drivers who are cars, a policeman who is directing the traffic at the corner of the street, and, a little further on, the same traffic being controlled by red and green lights: *hundreds of exigencies* rise up towards me: pedestrian crossings, notices and prohibitions; collectives ... instruments ... proclaiming with their frozen voices how they are to be used. ..."[5]

Implied in the notion of the practico-inert is technification. Technification structures human life through artificial determinations. It stands for ideational or physical acts which turn

[4] Ibid., pp. 304, 308.
[5] Ibid., p. 323.

against humanity. This aspect of technicality is consonant with Ellul's idea of *technique*.[6] It denotes a world of artifacts, humanly empowered, which ultimately determines human action. A milieu dominated by technique and by the practico-inert gives evidence of seriality, unreflection and necessity. In such a milieu human ends and means are pre-constituted.[7] In the environment of the practico-inert the core experience of culture consists of "doing unto things." The sense of being human comes from acting on matter, and the worked matter, in turn, designates everyone as the same, as mere Other. To speak of choices among technical milieus is wrong. For the technical milieu is generally the same everywhere; it transforms praxis into habit and forces human labor to trail behind it. Servitude to nature becomes servitude to technique whose first characteristic, as analyzed by Ellul, is artificiality. Neither Sartre nor Ellul uses these concepts as an abstract approximation of our reality. The struggle with the technical product as a social force is a concrete daily concern. Though the force originates from human activity this very activity becomes serial inertia, "counter finality," an anti-human force.

The experiencing of seriality is routine, since the practico-inert is the center of most of our social relations. Our daily encounters are mediated by worked materiality and objects. This mediation by means of things confers serial indifference upon us, which we recognize as passivity and diminished choice. It is the flight of our humanity into objects.

While it is obvious that the practico-inert permeates one's relationship to both the physical world and the cultural world, Sartre uses culture in a special meaning to refer to the domain of the ideal. Culture is the product of free and reflective praxis. It is the human struggle against the "impossible life" of seriality.

Seriality stands then for the fall of praxis. It stands for relations between *things,* and, therefore, is the inversion of au-

---

[6] Jacques Ellul, *The Technological Society,* trans. with an introduction by Robert K. Merton (New York: Vintage Books, 1964).

[7] Sartre, *Critique,* p. 325.

thentic human relations. However, since it is not a destiny, the individual may still revolt against it. Such an act of revolt is the property of the *praxis group*.

The struggle against the practico-inert: the praxis group

What follows is basically an anatomy of revolt. For purposes of enlivening description and analysis, Sartre uses a great number of examples drawn from historical data, all of which, however, are centered around events that took place during the French revolution (for example, the initial street skirmishes, the bloody civil war, the storming of the Bastille and so on). These historical events are not to be conceived of as a limiting case. The analysis is structural as well as historical and deals with the dynamics of every similarly related human group which desires to eliminate its seriality. While Sartre regards the serial group as the first order of sociality, followed by other types of group formations, he does not imply a necessarily chronological order to transitions between types. For example, the praxis group and the serial group may occur side by side in time. Transition from the one to the other is a social regularity. The sequential order of types of sociality illustrates the dialectic of historical continuity; what starts a praxis group as revolutionary is the negation of itself as inertia.

What follows is an organizational scheme of the stages through which a praxis group goes. The stages should not convey a rigid order in time; they are designed to make lucid and organized Sartre's highly rich but diversionary analysis.

The common threat. The experience of seriality is an offensive experience. Serial feelings like "isolation," "impotence" and "fear" stand for one's diminished capacity to choose. The experience of oppression, at this stage, relates to no particular object; it is instead a "free-floating" feeling of inadequacy. The person realizes that he is caught in a web of a rigid destiny, and at the same time that it is impossible for him to continue to submit to it any longer. The first prerequisite for change is this feeling of the offensive nature and the "impossibility" of the situation. The state of "impossibility" must be a state of danger for the individual, so as to constitute a condition that will force his liberating act. Hope alone cannot suffice, nor can a reflective position. The act which will change the situation originates from the "impossibility of the situation" itself. For human praxis at this stage must not be approached as the materialization of a plan, scheme or design to be contemplated at leisure.

The feeling of inadequacy or inertia does not come merely from the objective conditions of the practico-inert field, or from its technical contents, but from one's own action as an oppressed individual, who has been already pre-constituted by this field, these contents. The individual's action, in this oppressed context, is praxis in the negative sense. It is a human activity which has *interiorized matter* to become, for example, "the inhuman sentences which men have passed on men through worked matter." [8] Sartre attempts to establish that the origin of oppression is never an objective condition consisting of structures that are separate from humanity. Even scarcity, which is supposed to characterize an original objective relation between the human organism and the environment, does not reside in matter independently of man. "Scarcity reaches matter through man and man through matter." [9]

Sartre's point of emphasis is that the anti-human aspects of materiality are human in origin. The oppressed person's project to change the world is really a project of changing the adverse consequences generated by man. [10]

The force behind the desire to effect a change in the group is need. Need is the original state of tension in relation to nature. When we speak of integrated social life, need is brought about by any state of deprivation, on the condition that this state is recognized by everyone. Need can take the form of a

[8] Ibid., p. 332.
[9] Wilfrid Desan, *The Marxism of Jean-Paul Sartre* (Gloucester, Mass.: Peter Smith, 1974), p. 91.
[10] Sartre, *Critique,* p. 332.

struggle to survive physically, in which case it consists of warding off an external danger, an enemy, fighting a disease, an oppressor or other threat. It is this common deprivation of a collective which creates a common objective for praxis. The realization that the Other shares my need, as I do his, produces a state of enthusiasm; in other words, the universal character of deprivation leads to the discovery of one's Self in the Other. This is an important moment for the serial group, because the discovery that all Others share my destiny transforms "alterity," as my negative bond with them, into "quasi-reciprocity." The Other becomes the tool, not for the negation of the Self but for its affirmation. The Self recognizes its needs as being universal when it participates actively with Others in common praxis. For the serial group, cognitive of its needs, there is as yet no sense of organization, of consensus or even of an understanding of common purpose. The activity of the group is still *diffused* and *undifferentiated*. It originates essentially from the condition of the "impossible otherwise." Not only is there no organic unity to the group, the members themselves are not homogeneous and may come from diverse social origins. The only trait members of such a group share is a common threat, and the only revolutionary aspect is their sudden transformation from powerless members of a serial collective into a crowd.

The third person. Any concerted action by the serial group transforms it into a *group-in-fusion* (as in a demonstration, for example; but the nature of the act matters little here) and activates a new perception of the Self. The person ceases to be an Other, but nor is he yet a person with new individual objectives. The person, like everyone else, adopts a new non-passive orientation, but this new orientation still lacks *identity*. In this connection, according to Sartre, "[e]veryone reacts in a new way: not as an individual, nor as an Other, but as an individual incarnation of the common person." [11] Here the person is neither serial nor the member of a praxis group. He knows only that he is in a process of dissolving an old identity. He is no longer an "alterity." He experiences a new energy which leads to a

[11] Ibid., p. 357.

new bond. This new energy is the apprehension of the possibilities of freedom.

The dissolution of seriality does not immediately produce group unity, at least not in the sense of stability and organization. Each member of the group feels that he has the same share of rights, sovereignty and leadership as every other member. Each member becomes a "third person." He is neither the serial person nor the organized member of a collective totality. As a third person, he does not relate to the group, but mediates the group interaction, as he himself is mediated by everyone else. This *new* sense of reciprocal mediation is not based on comprehension of group power or hierarchy, but merely on the common purpose of the group as a whole. The Self in relation to the Other is the same as the Other in relation to the Self— a third party. As yet there are no symbols of affiliation, or tasks that lead to the division of labor. Any sense of integration comes from the dissolution of past identity, and the regarding of the present common praxis as a goal.

At this stage of social integration, the "subjective identity" is absent. Through the mediation of the group, every person ". . . is neither the Other nor identical (identical with *me*): but he comes to the group as I do, he is the same as me. The characteristic of the new, crucial structure of mediated reciprocity is this: that I *see myself come to the group in him,* and what I see is merely lived objectivity." Thus while the individual is spontaneously helping to create a group he is not doing so as a definite self-conscious subject. Everyone interiorizes the Other as objectivity. However, a new and sudden realization does occur. It rests on the fact that human beings, and not the mere commodities of the practico-inert, have become the center of this group formation. Mediation in the group comes to have a human component. The human world replaces, even if temporarily, the material world as the foundation of the group. This new world reveals itself in so far as every member is a "third person." The total group is identified not by an object lying beyond it, but by its self-oriented action. "The apparent *exis* of everyone (his being-there, immobile, in-the-midst-of-the-group) is revealed to me as *my praxis* both in me and in him . . . ; being in the group, in effect, consists in having come to it. . . ." [12]

All institutional and material aspects of the practico-inert are converted into single means for the practical ends of the individual (for example, the use of a building for a gathering). The commanding materiality which previously led to seriality is now appropriated as instrumentality by the human agent.

Non-Differentiation. Group formation and "regrouping" is carried out indiscriminately by the group-in-fusion. The regulatory function of such action is undifferentiated since it lacks an author. It is neither the product of an individual actor, nor the product of the group as a whole. In this connection, as Sartre writes, "the authorless words, repeated by a hundred mouths (including my own) do not appear to me as the product of the group . . . , but, in the act which comprehends it by actualizing its meaning, I apprehend it as the pure totalizing and regulatory presence of the third party (as *the same as me*) in so far as it accomplishes my integration where I am and *through my freedom.*" [13] For the group this is the moment of "immanence" which occurs before collectivization. This is the purest moment in human affiliation, the spontaneous moment of pure interiority which precedes all objectification by rules, rights, obligations, routines and so on.

An important question which has bearing on differences in approach between structural and existential positions is the weight which is assigned to the individual in affecting group behavior. The dominant approach in structural sociology speaks of a supra-organic quality of group life which is not reducible to its individual constituents (see Durkheim, for example). It is this supra-organic reality which constrains and determines individual behaviors. Sartre, however, rejects such a position as mystification. Sartre emphasizes that the group is a metamorphic form of the individual. This point will be elaborated in later sections. The group is an addition to the life of the existent individual. Addition is not mere summation but a quantity

[12] Ibid., p. 377.
[13] Ibid., pp. 380–81.

which, when interiorized, is perceived by the individual as the "size," or the presence of the group. Everyone in it counts. Size dissolves the number as a mechanical relation of exteriority and turns it into a feeling of power. Power becomes the product of the *presence* of everyone. The novelty of the size is the beginning of a sense of a group. But the size of the group is mere instrumentality, not in order to service abstract notions of group unity and group spirit, but in order to carry out concrete projects for the group. Sartre will not sacrifice the individual in the name of a group unity. The substance of the group at this stage is not unity, but its power as a means for a future goal. It is carrying out the task through every individual, which alone gives the group a sense of unity and intelligibility. No individual action is abstracted into the action of another, because "...*in praxis* there is no *Other,* there are only several *myselves.*" [14] Common praxis is not the product of a collective mentality, of a form of solidarity or of a contract; it is the spontaneous self-objectifying freedom of everyone.

The basic difference between the serial and the fused group is that the latter experiences co-essentiality and co-responsibility. The sense of power and sovereignty it experiences is shared by everyone. Egalitarianism is the rule in the fused group. The absence of tasks and projects makes leadership irrelevant at this stage. So to speak, "everyone" is the leader. One's action becomes an order for everyone, everyone being the common third person. The entire group feels responsible for each initiative and action. And the emerging sense of synthetic unity in the fused group comes from the transcending of the serial existence of the past.

In sum, what characterizes the fused group is its negation of the "impossible past." It throws off humiliations, powerlessness and mutual indifference. It fears mostly the return to the deadly obscurity and seriality of the past. The participants do not aim to organize themselves yet, but wish to remain ubiquitous. Ubiquity is maintained when action is continuous. It is this continuous action which most characterizes the fused group

[14] Ibid., pp. 394–95, 410.

and makes it intelligible to the outsider and to itself. There is also an element of violence directed against any trace of indifference or Otherness within the group, and, most importantly, directed against the endangering outside groups which perpetually threaten the newly gained sovereignty of self.

The pledge. When the fused group survives this initial stage of emergency, further reflection leads to a desire for permanency. Fervor subsides and the group faces the danger of dissolution. The already completed praxis becomes a memory of the past. Another danger is that the group will become its own end, engaging in indulgent recollections and analyses of its recent transformation. This is the danger of praxis turning into mere reflexivity. ". . . [R]eflexivity comes to the group from its past *praxis*. . . ." [15]

Moreover, the third person's role fades away. His practical task is cancelled. What continues to connect him with other members is a sense of pride and comradeship. But that is hardly a structure or a guarantee for the future. The absence of a project gives birth to propaganda and ideology as a group memory (such as in dramatic visits, marches, speeches and so on, at the site of a past action). Indeed, praxis loses its efficacy at the moment the object of its struggle is achieved. A real danger then faces the group: first, the possibility of the group moving into the practico-inert as a passive synthesis, but more gravely, the danger of a renewed seriality. The source of the danger is now internal.

Permanency becomes the group's objective. This new objective justifies differentiation, or the termination of the status of the third person. Unity, rather than praxis, becomes the aim. Praxis, originally directed against the common outside threat, is turned against the self. Praxis from now on leads to organization and differentiation. The group is ready to be organized, with the help of statutes and rights which serve as the foundation for permanence.

This is the stage of transition from praxis to routinization. It is at this level of integration that the social group is born. The

[15] Ibid., p. 415.

person needs the safety and guarantees of the group. But the need for guarantees also means dependency and the beginning of mistrust and suspicion. The specter of seriality re-emerges. This is the dramatic stage of the transition from fused group to a *pledge group.* The pledge is the group's guarantee against mutual betrayal. The fear of betrayal may not only be fear of the Other, but of one's own self as well. The possibility of a return to seriality brings about a psychological reorientation among group members: the members are ready now to surrender part of their freedom in favor of a pledge and a permanent group. The members need a surety against their own freedom, including the freedom to secede. The end of free praxis begins.

The pledge keeps the person from becoming mere Other to the rest of the group. It also leads to reciprocal protection against the terrible possibility of relapse into seriality and indifference. "... [M]y pledge becomes my surety for myself in that it is me offering myself, in every third party, as everyone's guarantee of not relapsing, in my person or through my conduct, into social alterity." [16] Moreover, by saying that the pledge introduces an element of mistrust into the group, Sartre is following the logic of *Being and Nothingness,* in which it is held that permanency is the negation of one's possibilities. The group becomes the limit of freedom.

In the fused group every person's action is identical to mine and the summing up of these actions leads to addition, group growth and a sense of intensified power. I act with my free praxis in the context of objective conditions that are the same for everyone. In this connection the unity of the group is factual and not symbolic. Here, unity is appropriate since there is still some perceived danger from the outside. I act in order to ward off the threat that could annihilate me, and the unity of the group is *instrumentally* necessary for my survival.

In the pledge group, in contrast, the unity of the group is symbolic and becomes an end in itself. The "play of signs and meanings" becomes important in itself and binds me to the Others. My freedom and its surety come from the Other. The

16 Ibid., p. 422.

Other limits his action as a pre-condition for my successful action. Thereafter, as Sartre says, "the project of limitation returns to him [through the pledge] as an exigency in him for everyone's freedom." [17]

The pledge introduces specialization and group differentiation. When I am certain of the action of the Other, I need no longer concern myself with his actions, and I can then concentrate on my own specialized task. In such a social arrangement my being in the group is not a free being and my behavior cannot be totally inventive, but constitutes itself as a function or necessity defined by the exigencies and demands of the situation.[18]

Permanence thus limits praxis. The pledge group is no longer capable of being transcended by any of its members. My action, for instance, does not radically affect the group. My betrayal of the group will only constitute a punishable act, and the unity of the group will not any longer depend on my willingness to remain in it.

The creation of the pledge group seems necessary because there is no guarantee that the group can actually fight back with the same fervor as in the past, in case of a renewed external danger. At this point, reflexive fear enters the group in the form of self-doubt. This is not a fear in *anticipation* of the danger, but a *lived* fear. "[This] reflexive fear is lived entirely *in the concrete*, through real facts: one man being exhausted, another wounded, and a third asleep, myself having an argument with a fourth, and so on." [19] To maintain alertness and a state of emergency the group begins to produce its own internal dangers. And, over time, internal dangers replace the real threat from outside, which has become diminished and is perceived as distant. The new internal danger is the horrible specter of relapsing back into seriality. The decreasing danger from outside is thus counteracted by the reflexive fear of losing the group itself.

---

[17] Ibid., p. 425.
[18] Ibid., p. 426.
[19] Ibid., p. 430.

Real dangers do not constitute the group any longer; the group maintains itself by internally reproduced anxieties.

The transition to the pledge group leads to the rise of violence. Violence appears in the group regardless of whether institutions of control, such as law and the police, have been developed or not. Death threatens every betrayal. The danger of group dissolution produces an artificial terror which is what gives rise to violence. But freedom is not diminished, for such violence requires free relations among group members engaged in a common action. "I have freely consented to the liquidation of my person as free constituent *praxis,* and this free consent returns to me as the free primacy of the Other's freedom over my own, that is to say, as the right of the group over my *praxis.*" [20] Violence serves as protection against the possibility of returning to seriality. It is protection and violence which constitute the pledge.

It matters little whether symbols of pledge are absent (for example, an oath, a flag, the Bible and so on) since the pledge at this stage is produced by a terror statute. The *statute* is the implicit right of everyone over everyone else. Terror, as the common statute, requires group violence. It becomes a relation of unity instead of separation.

As a result of the reciprocal relation between violence and protection, the bond of *fraternity* comes into being: ". . . [t]his fraternity is *the right of all* through everyone and over everyone." All punitive measures reaffirm the pledge and arouse the new bond of fraternity. Even ". . . [e]xterminating violence is . . . a link of fraternity between the lynchers and the lynched in that the liquidation of the traitor is grounded on the positive affirmation that he is *one of the group;* right up to the end, he is abused in the name of his own pledge and of the right over him which he acknowledged in the Others." Fraternity sets a limit on one's freedom, but the diminished freedom is also the newly willed identity. For the relation of fraternity is perceived as a bond of love. "[A]nger and violence are lived both as Terror against the traitor and . . . as a practical bond of *love* be-

[20] Ibid., p. 433.

tween the executioners. Violence is the very power of this lateral reciprocity of love." [21] The bond creates a system of closed and intense relations which characterize all authoritarian situations, intimate or collective. The more imagined the threat, the more violent the bond, which in turn creates a stronger intolerance toward deviations of any kind.

The power of terror is expressed by rudimentary forms of prohibitions, limits and inflexibilities. Indeed it is this elementary form of prohibition which constitutes the phenomenon of the sacred in the group, and may take the form of concrete things (such as sacred tablets, ceremonies, commemoration and so forth). The introduction of inert structures into the group begins. Sartre is not speaking of the rise of religion or culture, for as yet there are no conscious or programmatic deliberations by the group on these matters. The feeling of the sacred permeates the group as a "free-floating" sovereignty.

The pledge itself does not have to be a ceremonial action; it is a happening which occurs at the moment the group becomes its own end. Whenever permanency of the group becomes an end in itself, the group automatically and unceremoniously enters the stage of pledge. The previous homogeneity of the fused group now enters a stage of differentiation, where division of labor and allocation of tasks to be carried out outside the group territory become a daily reality. The individual transforms from a third person into a common individual. He approaches the stage of the organized group.

Laing's use of Sartrean concepts

One of the earliest and most successful applications of Sartre's ideas to areas of social concern is in Laing's work on mental illness and the family. Laing's analysis is particularly instructive since it stands as a practical application of Sartre's thought. While Laing adds nothing to the concepts *series* and *praxis*, his study of the family shows how the *Critique* can be applied to areas outside of the domain of philosophy.

[21] Ibid., pp. 438–39.

Laing's work centered around his view that mental illness is not an objective disease (process), but an act of choice (praxis). Of course, Laing, in this respect, had been preceded by Szasz,[22] who also considered mental illness to be action for which the ill person is responsible. Szasz condemned the patient for inappropriate behavior since he believed that the patient falsely appears to be helpless.

Laing considers aberrant behavior to be a volitional attempt to shake off what he calls the fixations of the ordering ego. With it the person tries to break away from the familiar and the sometimes false social self. But Laing does not subscribe to a theory of psychological health. There is no health model which ought to be restored, and this is precisely the meaning of anti-psychiatry. The idea of restoration of normality is absent in Laing's work since a model of normality is absent. Normality, in our social context, primarily implies a specific connection of relations with Others. Following Sartre's notion of *pledge* as a primary type of human relation, Laing contends that in modern culture the relations between Self and Other are shams since they are contaminated by the ambivalent attitudes of violence and protection. Alternative types of relationship, with less ambivalence, remain a mere hope for Laing, as they had been for Sartre. Laing's intellectual efforts take into account the fact that these alternative forms are now absent.[23]

In his early work,[24] Laing's breakthrough in psychiatry consisted of substituting existential concepts for conventional clinical ones. "Bad faith," "anguish" and "engulfment," for ex-

22 Thomas Szasz, *The Myth of Mental Illness* (New York: Dell Publishing Co., Delta Books, 1961).

23 R. D. Laing, *The Politics of Experience* (New York: Ballantine Books, 1967); see esp. p. 56.

24 See R. D. Laing, *The Divided Self* (1960; New York: Penguin Books, 1965). R. D. Laing and A. Easterson, *Sanity, Madness and the Family* (London: Tavistock Publications, 1961). Also Laing, in collaboration with D. G. Cooper, condensed in 1964 a translation of Sartre's major work in *Reason and Violence: A Decade of Sartre's Philosophy 1950–1960* (New York: Vintage Books, 1971). Laing's indebtedness to Sartre is acknowledged in most of his works.

ample, were observable in the clinic. They were supposed to make disturbed behavior comprehensible. Laing believed that the mentally ill had a comprehensible human experience, even if it was bizarre. Whereas schizophrenia had been looked upon by conventional psychiatry as an "objective" process in the individual, it was seen by Laing as an act of human intention. The choice and involvement of the subject in the behavior is based on a personal decision. Hence, in Laing, the passivity of Freudian determinism gives way to the responsible and active stance which characterizes Sartre's concept of the project.

Laing extended Sartre's ideas concerning schizophrenia from the individual to the family and brought them to fruition in *Sanity, Madness and the Family*. The basic theme of this work was epitomized in a short article published in 1962.[25]

Praxis, as we have seen, refers to intentional acts of the human subject which are oriented toward a goal. For this reason, praxis can be said to be a meaningful and intelligible event. It may be contrasted with process, which has no author and which occurs as an objective activity. Schizophrenia reflects praxis and not process, according to Laing. Process (which can be likened to the sociological concept of structure or to the scientific concept of a natural law) refers to an impersonal force, examples of which are "bureaucracy," "scarcity" and "class," but also social prejudices of all sorts. No one person can be the author or creator of a prejudice, a style or a class. Processes are divorced from the intentionality and responsibility of any single individual. When applied to the human situation, process denotes a serial group in which no person is essential and in which everybody is quantitatively interchangeable.

In a serial group each member denies that he is a member of that group and that any internal bonds exist with the others. This is a common behavior in instances of racial, sexual and other types of prejudice and discrimination.

In order to have actual group identity, interpersonal relations have to be accepted as necessary. Intimate interpersonal depen-

[25] R. D. Laing, "Series and Nexus in the Family," *New Left Review*, May/June 1962, pp. 7–14.

dence is Laing's notion of "nexus." Relations that are characterized by the nexus are typically family relations. Whereas series-
type relations indicate a human ensemble whose members share
some common object, goal or idea, even as they are independent
of each other, nexus-type relations constitute a group whose
members are unified through the interiorization of each other's
realities, interests, goals, and so on. The nexal group contains
inter-personal co-essentiality, loyalty and pledge. ". . . The nexus
exists only in so far as each person incarnates the nexus. The
nexus is everywhere, in each person, and is nowhere else than
in each. The nexus is at the opposite pole from the series. . . ." [26]

The pride or shame of each member of a nexal group depends
upon the attitudes of the other members of the group. There
can be no indifference in a nexal group. In such a setting, love
of the other is really the need for the other. One is loyal to the
other lest he be betrayed. The center of relation is love, but also
indebtedness. Betrayal or desertion is punished according to the
"nexus ethics," which is the emotional exile to the world of indifference or seriality. The nexal group (just as the praxis
group) has to invent "dangers" in order to continue to exist.
These "dangers" can be seen as an unfavorable world, in relation to which the family becomes a protective shield. Laing
explains the phenomenon of maternal over-protection on these
grounds. The price of protection from the external world, however, is internalized terror. Each person expects to control the
Other and to be controlled by the Other. Each person falls under
an ethic of reciprocal protection and is threatened with violence
if he steps out of line. A sense of security rests on need for each
other, it is the need to be needed by the Other. The nexal ethic
is based on tactics of enforced debt.

Laing denies to the nexal group (the primary group in sociological terminology) the attributes that functional analysis in
sociology usually attributes to such a group. In step with Sartre,
he attacks the organismic concept of the group, and specifically
of the family. The organic analogy cannot be extended to a multiplicity of persons without leading to mystification. The group

[26] Ibid., p. 12.

is not a totality of which the individual constitutes only a part; it is the sum total of individual *praxes*. The mood of the individual in a group, whether that of pride, sadness, inferiority or competence, is the result not of the general structure of the group as such but of the concrete behavior of another member in the group. For Laing, the conventional family, just as any pledge group, is a web of mutual relations of protection and terror. Socio-psychological states of distress and anxiety (including mental illness) are matters of communication, and what remains to be investigated is each person's perspective and each actor's stake in the given group situation.

Distressful feelings and inappropriate behavior are intelligible when we trace their impersonal "processual" character back to its individual source, that is, when we trace such phenomena back to the concrete behaviors of the members in the family. Processes, series, social institutions, families and so on appear incoherent and abstract, and become intelligible "when, and only when the steps in the vicissitudes of alienation from the praxis of each and every person can be retraced back to what at each and every moment is their only origin: ... the actions of each and every single person." [27]

[27] Ibid., p. 10.

six

Opposition

and identity:

the individual

and the group

The organized group

The analysis up until now has
dealt with the initial stages and types of group formation. What
distinguishes a member of the pledge group, for example, is his
membership *per se*. Membership in the pledge group is not differentiated by specific tasks or functions. It serves only to limit
one's freedom to betray the group. The danger of absolute freedom of group members creates a common need; the group must
consolidate itself. Consolidation comes into being in the form of
the division of labor. The division of labor is differentiation of
group members by function. It introduces the taking into consideration of relations of group members to things, or to the
outside world. Group organization leads to the distribution of
tasks in relation to the material environment. The process is
double-edged and takes two directions: the action of the group
upon itself and the action of the group upon the outside world.

The first aspect of organization comes about when the group
as a whole becomes an *object*. In the fused state, the individual
regards the group as an instrument. Each member is responsible
for bringing about group unity. But this unity is not by itself an
end; it was instead merely an instrument for serving immediate
and potential needs. In the pledge state, however, group unity
becomes an end in itself; it is threatened by every member in so
far as each member threatens to bring about a relapse of seri-

ality. In this case, each person ceases to be an *additive power* and becomes a *negative power*. This negative power takes the form of relational reciprocities of terror-love or violence-protection. In the organized stage, the group member becomes a *function*. Function serves as a concrete limit to the person's diffuse sense of power, and it sets boundaries to his possible types of action. *Function,* as a new link between group members, is somewhat different from the link of *primitive terror* in the pledge group. But the basis of functional relations is still terror. Function differentiates the members, introduces alterity to the group and creates a hierarchy among types of praxis and membership. At this stage it can be said that the individual belongs to the group in so far as he carries out a specific task.[1] Terror, in this context, operates as a particularization of one's freedom through a function. But the person carries out his tasks freely, as he did the pledge, since his function is comprehended as *both* his right and his duty.

Though function partially replaces terror, terror can always reappear whenever the historical circumstances of the group are conducive to it, as in the cases of revolt, labor strikes or social transformation.

The second aspect of organization occurs because function can be defined only in relation to tools in the material surrounding. Function, in this context, is a technical relation between a group member and an instrument. The instrument designates positions in the group. It is, in fact, this relation between individuals and the tools assigned to them through functions which creates the practico-inert, or the practical field of the group members. It also determines the manner in which a member will be integrated into the group. Sartre refers to this as the mediating moment of organic praxis.[2] In this manner, external relations to objects determine internal relations between members of the group.

While pledge stood for the negation of alterity—that is, for

---

[1] Jean-Paul Sartre, *Critique of Dialectical Reason,* trans. Alan Sheridan-Smith, ed. Jonathan Ree (London: NLB, 1976), p. 449.

[2] Ibid., p. 463.

the forbidding of Otherness—in the organized group, alterity is induced and created. It comes about when the Other is defined through his task. Inner "qualities" of the person cease to be relevant. His tasks are designated by the particular needs of the group, as part of its relation to the practico-inert. By means of a convention or a rule the person's alterity is intelligible to everyone. But alterity does not bring about alienation as yet. For this is different from the serial situation. In seriality, I do not understand, Sartre says, why my neighbor is another; for alterity appears as accidental. In the organized group, on the other hand, alterity is introduced as a practicality. In fact, alterity or Otherness becomes necessary in order to carry out the group's aim or common task. Alterity introduces concrete forms of social relations and clarifies the differences between group members. Sartre puts it this way: "At the level of the organization, being-in-the-group is no longer an abstract, polyvalent determination of human relations; it is the organized relation which unites me to each and all." [3] Alterity becomes the basis of a new and higher unity. It determines hierarchies, levels of competence, skills and so on, so as to facilitate the completion of a concrete task.

Fraternity does not disappear at this stage, but is conceived by the members as group heterogeneity. Each person (whether as a soldier, farmer, worker or intellectual) is my equal as long as his function helps me carry out mine in the context of the group aim. Fraternity contains an aspect of reciprocity. It contains a concrete set of relationships, more complex and richer than the original bond in pledge affiliation. In the *fused group* everyone was a third person and reciprocity was a direct and lived relationship. In the *pledge group,* reciprocity continued to exist, but with elements of constraint and inertia. It set limits to my possibilities. Constituted by relations of protection and violence, it revealed a bond with an absent Other, rather than with a concrete Other. It served as a form of protection against "the separating power of inert materiality." [4] In the *organized group* reciprocity comes to the group from without, from materiality itself,

[3] Ibid., p. 466.
[4] Ibid., p. 471.

as the practical relation between humans and things, and it is manifested through the differential effects of function.

Analytic rationality and synthetic rationality

Sartre calls social structure the "inorganic skeleton" of an organized group. It stands for sets of prescriptions and prohibitions which stabilize social relations among group members. It takes the form of rights and duties, and permeates the group in the form of the normative suppositions which guide the action of group members. Anticipation of punishment, ostracism or reward demonstrates the silent presence of these suppositions. But structure does not bear a real resemblance to certain conceptions prevalent in sociological theory. For example, it is not identical to the generalized Other of Mead or the collective conscience of Durkheim. Sartre would oppose these collective designations and would regard them as alienating abstractions, unintelligible to the real individual. He criticizes "structural reason" which operates with these abstractions and which confers upon them a life ostensibly independent of human praxis and individual consciousness. He attacks the theoretical reduction of the individual's initiative to such inorganic structural conceptions.

For Sartre, the human individual is at the beginning of each and every social phenomenon. He is the author of free and spontaneous praxis as well as the basis of inertia. The individual pledges his life to the group; and in all transformations, he remains the author of all social products. Social structure is not a behavior; it is the product of an analytical rationality which becomes intelligible through individual action only.

There are two aspects of structure which can clarify its general meaning. The first has to do with the fact that it is the *potential field* for the acts of the individual. The second has to do with the fact that it serves as the individual's *means* for arriving at a certain end. In the first instance, a person's relations with the others (rights, duties, limitations and prohibitions) define his objective field in terms of the amount of power he possesses to act in a certain way. In the second instance, social structure, as an instrument, is the means by which potentia is actualized.

It is upon integration of these two aspects that a certain act or behavior becomes meaningful for the individual. To act meaningfully is to possess knowledge of the *power* and the *means* that are made available to the person in the context of group life. This means that social structure stands for the "idea which the group produces of itself." [5] It relates to its field of practical actions, its relations between part and whole, its instruments, its qualities and its power. In fact, social structure, in this practical sense, serves as the basis for the group *ethic,* which prescribes common tasks and reciprocal relations on the basis of its self-image. The self-image, or the self-idea, of the group does not, however, possess a magical or hyper-organic quality. It is a product of the group's material organization and of human praxes. Individual loyalty to a set of group-related principles and objectives, which constitute the group idea, is not blind, but is the product of an original act of loyalty founded on the *pledge.* The group idea is crucial for the shaping of the outlook and judgment of group members. But such outlook and judgment is above all a property of the common individual. It is the product of his *free act* and his *pledge.*

In the analysis of social structure as means, the idea of instrumentality refers to inertia. Both the material and the human fields become means that are quantifiable, predictable and manageable. Every person becomes a calculable element in order to facilitate analytical rationality of social forms as though they were independent of human praxis. Analytical rationality is subordinated to the synthetic or integrative process of individual acts of totalization. The givenness of the group is not analytical or logical, but factual. The continued existence of the group is made possible through the praxis of each group member. Analytical rationality, in the form of group rules and regulations, is subordinated to synthetic totalizations and may be shattered by deviant acts. Analytic rationality is vulnerable and is often

[5] Ibid., p. 499.

transcended by concrete human choices in the form of individual action.

The opposite, however, is not true. One cannot transform concrete human interdependencies into an abstract representation, statistic or diagram. If one succeeds in doing so it is done only with great artificiality. A quantification of human social reality is a mystification of the actual situation. It is done for the purpose of making the real object comprehensible from the outside. This is possibly what the social scientist does, since he considers the analytical property as the only proper method of getting at the group's real being. Analysis on the part of the researcher and understanding on the part of the reader are both given in terms of exteriority. It is the explaining of the insider's pattern of social relations to an outsider or stranger. The task of the social scientist who is making the explanation "is not a matter of projection or transposition: he is simply creating an inert object which presents in exteriority, to a man from the exterior, a set of passive characteristics, which retain only the inertia of these [social] structures. . . ." [6] Social structure, in this sense, is reduced to what Sartre refers to as *ossature*. A structure-ossature is an empty representation, incapable of getting at the complex knowledge which is given in the silent dimension of the group's inner life. The meaning of social action inevitably escapes the outsider-researcher.[7]

Individual action and group action

In contrast to individual action, the term *group action* often seems obscure. Individual praxis is intelligible. With it one can perhaps explain the transitions from the fused group to the pledge group and eventually to the organized group. But while no critical problems are encountered in the analysis of these transitions, Sartre feels that a major question was suppressed, nevertheless. The question is about the character and conditions of group action, and the extent of its intelligibility. When we

[6] Ibid., p. 503.
[7] Ibid., p. 501.

say "they stoned the Bastille" we speak of the subject in the plural and the action in the singular. It can be asked: "How does it come about that I understand the meaning of a group action?" This is what Sartre refers to as the "constituted dialectic," or the problem of the practical individual comprehending the action of an organized collective. Certain group-related events may not be produced or even understood from the position of the isolated individual. The collective act of pledge itself is an example. Does this imply that a Gestalt or hyper-consciousness exists in the group, which the individual merely lives out or concretizes? Sartre's answer to this difficult question is that the individual is the model for the group, and that *the group is the metamorphic form of individual praxis*. Group action is undoubtedly far richer than individual action. Yet, it remains homogeneous with it. Sartre insists that group action sets itself objectives and achieves them through operations that are individual in character.[8] Individual praxis is the point of reference for all collective action and its comprehension.

Certain groups are formed in order to carry out objectives that no single person can carry out. But these objectives could have been conceived by several unconnected individuals. They can even be discovered by serial individuals isolated from each other. According to Sartre, "[t]here is no common aim that an individual cannot set himself, *provided* that, in the unity of the project, he tries to constitute a group to realize it." Thus, the sovereignty of individual praxis remains intact, and the constitution of the group is initially given over to the individual, not as idea or as Gestalt, but as a means to achieve an objective. In this manner the group is made comprehensible to the individual. Comprehension is not a mental faculty independent of the already completed act. It is contemporaneous with the act and reveals itself in the understanding which accompanies the act. Moreover, the person comprehends the action of the group because he understands his own action. "This implies, therefore, that common action and individual *praxis* exhibit a real homogeneity. The individual would be unable to understand either

---

[8] Ibid., p. 510.

his own common action in terms of the totalizing *praxis* of the group, or that of a group external to himself, if the structures of common *praxis* were of a different order than those of individual *praxis*. If the objectives of the group had a hyper-individual character, then the individual could never be able to grasp them." [9] The objectives that the group sets and the common operations which are used to achieve them are individual in character, Sartre concludes.

There is no ideological reason to emphasize the individual instead of the group. Sartre claims that such a conclusion is an accidental by-product in his reasoned analysis. However, the point which he constantly makes is unequivocal: *the group, in the mind of the individual actor, is an object that is interiorized by personal praxis as an instrument, and it is made intelligible by the individual's goal.* The group becomes a group-object, a means for objectification like any other means in the field.

In Sartre's example of a group in an emergency, the Others in the group become plural amplifications of the individual. They are means of avoiding danger. They perform for him a task which he would have had to perform successively.[10] It is this *simultaneity* of action carried out by many persons which introduces the novelty of the group to the individual.

The character of the collective is therefore understandable, not as an objective reality, but as a product of individual praxes. The comprehension of the group and of individual praxis is virtually the same. Such comprehension is made possible because the act on both levels is aimed toward a goal. In translating the goal—from the future to present—the person is able to comprehend his individual praxis as well as group action.

Individual praxis as a model

The creation of an integrated and closely knit collective is a universal human aim. The *integrated group* is frequently described by historians in their work on certain types of groups, meetings

[9] Ibid., pp. 509, 511.
[10] Ibid., p. 514.

and activities, especially revolutionary ones. They describe all-powerful and organic totalities in which individuals dissolve and then reappear as part of a "We" or "Us." Alliances between different social groups (soldiers, peasants, workers) are depicted as Gestaltist syntheses which sweep away division and conflict. These alleged syntheses, according to Sartre, are representations of the physical principle of quantity becoming quality, which Sartre condemns as an exterior dialectic imposed on humanity. A unified group takes place on the basis of internal commitments occasioned by the pledge. But the pledge, if we will remember, is a link of fraternity-terror or violence. Violence is the foundation for such a group, whether it originates in a democratic or a totalitarian manner. Violence accompanies all stages of group integration and unification. And it becomes more pronounced as the group moves away from the original simple pledge. Fraternity ends as violence becomes organized and institutionalized.[11] In the transition from the pledge group into the organized group, the third person disappears. The third person embodied a short and pure moment of social reciprocity and stood for spontaneous mediation devoid of terror. In the later stages of integration, the third person disappears and group members take on the roles of common individuals. These later developments are based on constraint.

But whatever level of integration the group achieves, its internal life and character never transcend individual praxis. This may appear paradoxical, since a group is different than an individual. The group doubles and multiplies the strengths and talents of each separate member but it cannot reproduce him, contends Sartre. It will never possess a Gestaltic or organic quality that transcends the individual *model of action.* Sartre gives us an example of the man-hunt to illustrate this. When hunting for a fugitive, the hunters only emulate the ideal of individual action. From the point of view of the individual being tracked, the group appears as a single ferocious individual. He apprehends the group members as united through their one goal, which is to capture him. In mentally representing the group's

[11] Ibid., pp. 521, 523.

action the individual reconstructs it as the action of one person with different organs. The presence of group members behind a tree or a wall is likened to the presence of an individual. He comprehends the hunt through the model of individual action. Certainly, no single person can achieve what this group can achieve. To imitate a formation of guards, says Sartre, "one would have to have eyes all around one's head, and arms in one's back; to resemble a combat unit which is protected by guards at night, one would have to be able to sleep and watch at the same time." [12] The point is not to deny the reality of group life, but to emphasize its homogeneity with the life of the individual.

The group appears, therefore, as a metamorphic extension of individual praxis. It is like a machine imitating the various capacities of the person. But, regardless of how it may be organized, it is denied the element of conviction which accompanies the human act. One is awed by its overpowering presence and differentiated functions. Leaders come into being, orders are obeyed and functions are distributed. But the group only points out the individuals which exist within it. "The group is an individual conception."

Durkheim's concept of the *collective conscience* points to a solidarity external to group members yet collectively guiding their actions. Durkheim's notion is reviewed by Sartre and criticized. For Sartre, the concept of agreement of minds, which he criticizes, refers to the common base of different group members along with their interests and functions. It can be called consensus. It may be a solution to a problem within a group in which there are numerous interests and individual perspectives. Here, we speak of reciprocities, coordination and cooperation among sub-groups and group members. Leaders, organizers, committees and subcommittees come into being. The individual is dissolved and in certain circumstances anonymous. But regardless of the means used to arrive at the solution, the solution is the creation of individuals. Proposals might be changed or amended, but they are changed or amended by one or another

[12] Ibid., p. 524.

individual. If an agreement is arrived at, it is certainly not the same as that which characterizes the agreement of two scientists with respect to a scientific law. The solution is not universal but rests on the unity of the particular group. Everyone is the same and identical with respect to its adoption. The solution confers a common structure to group life which every member obeys. The common agreement inheres in everyone as an "omnipresent inertia," which liquidates each personal position and imposes itself as a limit to action. The common solution or agreement is a *common inertia* adopted by the group as a whole, though the solution was originally the product of individual praxes, that is to say, the product of different proposals suggested, amended and contradicted by individuals.[13]

The inertia which negates individual praxis and elevates it to a higher level is a necessary condition for group action. It is through this negation and elevation that the individual becomes a function, or a *common individual.* But in spite of the fact that the individual is no longer an isolated individual, the constituted group remains as *his* rational means.[14] The unity which he helps to give it, by giving himself up to it, is not fixed as "a coin which has been struck." Its rationality remains synthetic, constituted by him and subject to change.

In this connection, the group is a "worked thing," or product, containing inert determinations. It continues to strive toward the organismic ideal of a group but never realizes it. The organismic ideal becomes a regulatory idea in relation to which the group arranges and structures itself without achieving its real aim. The group "remains a *totalization,* and a being which is subsidiary to the practical organism, and [it remains] one of its products." [15]

Praxis and process

Sartre contends that inertia in the group is equivalent to *process*. Inertia is that aspect of the group life which can be statistically

13 Ibid., p. 536.
14 Ibid., p. 537.
15 Ibid., p. 539.

quantified. Differences between process and praxis are like differences between the act of the *organic individual* and the *inert structure* of the group. Praxis is revealed by the *end* of action. It constitutes a project. It has a specific author. It mediates past, present and future. Process is the numerical aspect of a collective (given in percentages, rates, quantifiable aspects of differentiation, and other averages.) It is a collective characteristic, which may include the individual in so far as he is a member of the collective. To comprehend process, one refers to supra-individual qualities which are artificially produced in pure exteriority such as charts and diagrams. Process makes every group into an object, and every member in the group into a being outside himself, that is to say, the group becomes a reality toward which the person is always an outsider. Process refers to laws as revealed in pure exteriority. General sociological analysis uses the concept of process to represent the life of the group. Here, the group appears as an inert thing pushed toward its destiny and containing no individual authority or responsibility. In artificial imitation of the properties of the living organism, we see it move and evolve from growth to aging, to death and so on.

General theoretical sociology[16] sees in these processes a mystifying "objectivity" that is depicted as an extraordinary, and virtually unintelligible, quality of group life. Sartre does not deny the existence of such processes, but he insists that they are intelligible since they are products of human praxis. Praxis, once completed, produces its own inertia. In moving from the spontaneity of the first act of free praxis, it creates a quantifiable property that is rationally analyzable. When actions are multiplied, a serial and quantitative group status is produced, which is what a collective desires to extract from the isolated individual operation. It is this inert quality that characterizes group action. There is no ontology to this group praxis, only individuals practically organizing themselves as *means* for a common aim. If the intelligibility of the constituted action is difficult, it is because multiplied individual praxis are used instrumentally

[16] Sartre cites the works by Levine, Kardiner, and Moreno.

to appear common, while in fact they are individual.[17] The negation of individual praxis as a discrete entity occurs in all cases, in so far as everyone takes the group to be an instrument. The multiplicity of actions becomes an interiorized feature of the individual's life. It is the means by which he estimates his power and options.

Every group operates as both praxis and process. Praxis is comprehended upon understanding the objectives of the group in question. Process is comprehended when the group is seen as an instrument. For it is then that process operates as a quantity and as a feature of the general field of the practico-inert.

Sartre uses a simple example to illustrate the invariable concomitance of praxis and process. Referring to two groups of combatants, he says: "[T]he hostile group . . . determines the enemy both as *praxis* and as process. It cannot actually be unaware of the enemy *praxis* as such; it must comprehend and anticipate it on the basis of its aim; but at the same time, if it wishes to prevent it from being achieved, it must strike the enemy at the level at which *praxis* is also the development of process (destroying its supply-bases, cutting its lines of communication, etc.)."[18]

Praxis and process, like *pour-soi* and *en-soi,* constitute the dialectics of self-production. I produce myself both as subject and as object. My first act of disengagement from seriality is an act of creative and free praxis. But in order to secure my new freedom, I limit this freedom (as the property of everyone) with pledges and commitments. This creates inert group determination. The same is true of the historical development of social forms, where we find a movement from freedom to inertia, from charisma to routinization, and so on.

The group-for-the-other

No group exists independently of other entities and groups. Group-identity is not self-sufficient. The social space which it

[17] Sartre, *Critique,* p. 557.
[18] Ibid., p. 557.

occupies is sometimes shared by other groups. This new perspective of approaching the group from the vantage point of the other group is part of Sartre's effort to see the group in dialectical terms. The group is seen as constituting itself in both the practical internal praxis and in the reactions to it from outside.

Sartre turns to the "non-grouped" social formations and uses their reactions and relations to the group as a background for analysis. This approach was already pointed out in *Being and Nothingness*. There, the Other is the background for understanding the Self. Intelligibility does not reside in the object of analysis alone. In the present context, the Other *vis-à-vis* the group may be anyone outside the group: a customer, a researcher or an indifferent observer. Sartre uses the post office as a concrete example of a group that is organized and differentiated. The customers of the postal service are the Others to the group, who constitute a non-grouped element. The postal clerks are viewed by the customer as members of an organized group. They appear as practico-inert aspects of the post office, as much as the postal boxes. From a theoretical point of view, there is no distinction to be made between the clerks and the mail boxes. What is viewed by the customer is the simple unity of people and instruments, of praxis and process. The field of the practico-inert in this case appears united and is not reducible to either the activity of the clerks or to the instruments. The distinction between clerks and instruments is perceived, in fact, as inessential. The clerks and instruments are merely specifications *produced* by a group founded on a common professional oath. In the mind of the customer the entire group appears to be involved in the activity of dealing with the mail. What distinguishes a specific clerk is not particular praxis, but personal characteristics such as courtesy, clumsiness or cleanliness. Even a personal acquaintance with the clerk does not change the customer's perception.

The customer as Other attaches an objective quality to this group. The clerks appear as a group-object, defined by their aims. It is from this angle of the group, as an object, that the customer meets with and comprehends the particular clerk intersubjectively. "[T]his intersubjectivity [as objectivity] does not relate to any abstract or 'collective' consciousness: it is quite simply the reflexive structure of the group as seen by the user." The inessentiality of the clerk is given in his own activity as a person merely working on behalf of the group. But he loses his essentiality precisely at that moment at which he is identified as a member of the group. The mediation on the part of the customer, as Other, turns the simple activity of the clerk into an expression of a fixed totality.[19] Without his group status, the clerk appears to the customer not only as a mere Other, but also as an isolated Other. The isolation is intensified by the fact that the clerk is set apart from the rest of his group in a "forest of humanity"—the density of all the others that are not his group. No group can possibly retain one space as its permanent unifying container. The end result is the prominence of the *absent* group as the object for recognition and comprehension, and the diminution of the *present* individual clerk as but its inessential detail.

The Other and his reactions can bring about additional processes in the comprehension of the group. We are all familiar with attitudes of hostility or sympathy which are directed at parties, movements or cults through a particular representative. The representative *vis-à-vis* the outside group desires to appear as distinct from his individual characteristics (such as particular level of intelligence, background, competence and so on). He desires to appear the same as all the other members of his particular group. These changes in his self-conception are not the product of inclination or initiative. They are required of every member in the group as he faces other groups. When confronting the Other he becomes an inert mouthpiece of consciousness, since he repeats the empty contents of the debate, and since he reproduces the image of the party or the movement as a group-totality. He represents it as an analytical structure which is "frozen" and "ossified," rather than as an active praxis. It is the presence of the serial Others, as the opposition, which brings about such changes in him, and along with them, brings about *unintelligibility*. He no longer grasps or relates to his group as

[19] Ibid., 570.

an active being, full of initiative and praxis, but relates to it as it appears to the Others. The group is comprehended as an object which re-creates itself everywhere as the same group. At that conjuncture he is deprived of the only thing which can be used for genuine comprehension—his individual praxis. Without it, he not only ceases to comprehend his own position, but the real position of the other members of his group as well. His action is no longer brought about as means with the group as its end, but instead "he produces it through the mediation of the Other as the controlling schema of his relations to the Other." He experiences his relation to the group as a relation of *exteriority*. He relates as an object instead of as an individual. This is the image of the group as it is produced by the Other, which becomes his shelter and his defense.[20]

This new transformation of his innermost being and of his group can never happen to him as long as he is an active member of the group. It may only happen when he, as a member of the group, is seen by the Other, *studied* by the Other or confronted by the Other. The qualities of a fixed totality, or of an object, or of a supra-individual entity, are qualities produced not by the concrete and constituent praxis of group members, but, so to speak, from the *outside,* from the position of the antagonistic *Other,* or they are produced by the sociologist, or even by the indifferent everyday observer.

On entering once again into the midst of his group, this object-reality, however, disappears. It disappears along with the disappearance of the *Others.* Mediation ceases to occur by means of the Other. But he also realizes that it is impossible for him to surrender to the group absolutely. For the group cannot be a totality-subject either. It cannot retain an autonomous position or a *consciousness of its own.* This paradox which results in the notion of "impossible integration" leads us to the topics of *institution* and *authority.*

[20] Ibid., pp. 573–75.

seven

The

problem of

authority

        If the group possesses no imma-
nent basis for cohesion, and if it has no internal "viscosity"
save its existence as an extension of individual praxis, then the
issue of group authority becomes critical and important. Moreover, since no one is completely sovereign in the group, no one
is totally the group; that is to say, the mere coming into being
of a leader does not solve the problem of authority. This is
where the concept of *institutionalization* is relevant.

    In the fusion group, I have noted that every praxis in the
form of the third person regulator represented sovereignty.
There was no authority external to the *fusion group*. The action
of each member was spontaneous, to which everyone else related in a continually restructuring fashion. When the pledge
was introduced, it was done so because the equal sovereignty
of all Others could mean betrayal and group dissolution. We
analyzed the pledge as an instrument of group terror. It was
generated by mistrust and suspicion. It protects the group as a
whole instead of the individual. Through the pledge, the unity
of the group emerged. But this new unity was only considered
as a mere means by which division of labor, or differentiation
of tasks, could come about without apprehension.[1]

    With the transition to the next level of group formation,

[1] Jean-Paul Sartre, *Critique of Dialectical Reason,* trans. Alan
Sheridan-Smith, ed. Jonathan Ree (London: NLB, 1976), p. 581.

that of the organized group, the notion of function was introduced. It was supposed to lead to a set of social relations capable of being quantified and measured—"a skeleton of relations capable of being treated by an ordinal calculus," [2] according to Sartre.

But these stages of group totalization cannot guarantee complete integration at the levels of both action and meaning, which the group desires. The pledge or organized *relations* render the parts interchangeable and turn the person into a *common individual,* but they do not guarantee cohesion. Cohesion is demanded by the group since it is uneasy when facing the "forest of serial humanity." The creation of group cohesion becomes an apparently necessary and continuous group operation.

Moreover, in serving the group, the individual frequently leaves the group's territory. Initiative, representation in the outside world, and so on, render spatial co-presence impossible. The group therefore faces the danger of dissolution in two ways: seriality from without (brought about by exposure to the Other), and seriality from within (embodied in the innovative praxis of the individual). Initiative and risk-taking for the sake of the group may ironically become a menace. It may produce suspicion, and may call for the periodic *purges,* which, however, cannot destroy free praxis completely, for individual praxis is capable of reorganizing and reasserting itself. In order to govern group life, certain social formations curtail free praxis and promote passive alterity.[3]

Passive alterity in this context differs from the serial inertia which characterized the group in the early stages of its existence. Passive alterity is the result of a collective operation, a "systematic petrification" of individual initiative in favor of a common regulative practice. This operation is meant to reconcile the ontological unity of the group, which is abstract, with a practical unity which is based on individual action.[4] It is at this level that we find the process of institutionalization. Terror,

2 Ibid., p. 582.
3 Ibid., p. 598.
4 Ibid., p. 599.

which abolishes individual freedom, consolidates group authority. The individual retains his function but the group appropriates his initiative and freedom for its own ends. In the process
of institutionalization, two transformations take place: the first
is the sanctification of inertia and the second is the acceptance
of general authority.

The sanctification of inertia

The impotence of the common individual influences the formation of institutions. Serial impotence emerges as a new type of
relation in the group, based on the essentiality of the group
and on the inessentiality of the individual person. The emerging
collective body does not desire to change and feels threatened
by it. The sense of importance and power that the member of
the organized group feels is tolerated in the group to the degree
that his praxis no longer brings about change. Proposals for
change, which may result from the advanced heterogeneity of
functions, only lead to mistrust. A desire for new projects appears as a negative determination and is regarded with suspicion and fear. Initiative falters, for "I do not know with what
alterity it [the new plan] will be affected: it will be deformed
and diverted, and there is a danger that it will bring about
results quite contrary to those I intended; it may damage the
common object of the common practice (at least, as I discover
it in my experience); or it may be turned against me to destroy
me. And this very concrete reason always tends . . . to plunge
me even deeper into silence." Every act of individual initiative
has this danger of divisiveness because in it there is a "glimpse
of one's freedom." And so institutional inertia becomes intensified by means of separation and non-involvement. In fact, as
soon as the group feels that it is powerless to effect changes
short of complete disruption, it has become an institution.[5]

Sartre does not deny that the institution is useful, either for
the individual or for certain subgroups within it. For just like
the organized group, it protects rights and offers means. Its

[5] Ibid., pp. 601–02.

being and strength, however, come about not as a result of freedom and conscious praxis, but from "emptiness, from separation, from inertia and from serial alterity." [6]

In the organized group the person experienced his rights as the right to do his duty. On the institutional level, rights demand recognition. Recognition, however, is risky, and constitutes a challenge for the group since the power it involves must not reside in any particular individual. Recognized power denotes freedom and autonomy which must be suppressed. The individual therefore renounces any expression of individual ego-centered competence or freedom, in order to sustain the unity and inert stability of the group. This renunciation is a process through which a "systematic self-domestication of man by man" takes place.[7] The end result is the creation of tamed men who will be essentially defined by their relationships to the institution, that is to say, the institutionalized man. Inertia is sanctified. Everybody is implicated in this arrangement, an arrangement which will eventually become the property of future generations.

The acceptance of authority

Sartre treats authority as a human activity. Authority is not a structure or a group of regulations, but is the product of a concrete individual or subgroup fulfilling a function for a particular purpose. Denied any basis other than human praxis, authority does not represent a collective conscience, or any supra-human agency. Nothing is sacred about it. "[S]overeignty is man himself as action, as unifying labor, so far as he has a purchase on the world and is able to change it." [8]

Authority is given in the right of the individual to act, a right which extends over all other individuals as well. Because this right is the property of everyone, authority is tempered by reciprocity. The best example of such reciprocity occurs in the fused group where authority is exercised as co-authority, where

6 Ibid., p. 603.
7 Ibid., p. 606.
8 Ibid., p. 610.

each person serves as a "co-sovereign"—either in terms of means or ends—for everyone else. In the fused group authority is exercised as quasi-authority. It is a product of praxis and is shared equally by all. In the fused group it is not something abstract, sacred or supra-individual. Even when it becomes group authority, it does so through the free and common act of the pledge oath.

Sartre is not particularly concerned with the historical emergence and development of authority. He aims to deal with the formal conditions that presuppose it, conditions that become most pronounced in the institutional setting.

Sartre studies authority as it is exercised by the institutionalized group. A principal characteristic of institutional authority is leadership. Such leadership occurs when an institutionalized group regulates the activity of serial groups in the community. In fact, such non-charismatic leadership is defined with respect to seriality. Leadership and authority could not emerge, for example, in the fused or praxis groups, since they are active and self-determined, in the sense that each member acts as a third person regulator. With respect to the institution, leadership performs the inverse function of the third person regulator, since it coordinates and authorizes all regulators. Sartre is not alluding to charismatic types of leadership. He is dealing with institutional leadership which is delegated rationally by a statute, and carried out by a government, a committee or a subgroup. Initiative, planning and other organization measures need not always originate with the leaders, but usually pass through them so as to return to the group as a new command. This occurs at the expense of the common individual who is divested of his status as the mediator of "all through all." The "lost power" is turned back against him as a command from an Other. Obedience to the command is carried out under constant threat of *legitimized violence*. Disobedience would mean a return to seriality. By refusing dissolution he legitimizes violence as a common repressive measure. Repression becomes the everyday means of group integration and cohesion.[9]

9 Ibid., pp. 613, 630.

Sartre does not deal with the command and with obedience along the lines of the master-slave relation. The subject matter is not that of absolute authority which creates its own institutions. He views society as modern, legal and rational. Its leaders are representatives of the institutional system itself, with its whole apparatus of laws and regulations. He deals with "institutional men" who represent authority from "the outside" and who indicate a turning point in the development of human group formation. This is the point at which autonomous praxis turns into passivity and inertia. The individual who receives commands does not regard the leader as a constraining or manipulative individual, but as a fully legitimate social actor. The individual (as citizen) recognizes the decline of the original synthesis which originated in the praxis group. He is aware of the serial separation and silence that result from institutional relations. And this dangerous state, when it does not lead to a revolt, is counteracted by the fact that he views institutional authority as "a systematic and ordered deployment of the original synthesis." [10]

In the master-slave relation, as conceived by Hegel, the slave does not regard his master's command as legitimate, even if he obeys it. In contrast, the institutionalized individual sees constraint as a means to an end. *Institutional authority* gains its legitimate character from this act of *willing obedience* on the part of the institutionalized person. The freedom of the individual is renounced in favor of what is regarded by him as a communal praxis, even if this communal praxis exists "as an abstract, negative object of an empty intention." [11] In the process, authority becomes ambiguous since it is considered both individual and collective. Enforced or cynical obedience (as in a master-slave relationship) would indicate a crisis and would probably lead to the overthrow of authority and to a new cycle of reorganization and group formation.

Individual freedom ceases with the emergence of the institution, but it remains active in the leader, who alone can embody

---

[10] Ibid., p. 620.
[11] Ibid., p. 620.

the principle of independence. He remains in everyone as the *Universal Other*. He produces the illusion of ontological or biological unity, and creates a synthetic activity in a group which would otherwise tend toward dispersion. Here lies the source of the group's ambivalent attitude toward authority: while it decays as a result of inert institutionalization, it nevertheless regards the institutional person as an agency of integration. "... [L]iving and one, he [the leader] reveals common unity to the half-dead group as a symmetrical synthesis of the human body." This does not mean, however, that the group judges the institutional leader naively. It means that through him, the members relieve themselves of their mutual mistrust with the understanding "that he [the institutionalized leader] will express everyone's mistrust of everyone." [12]

In sum, the institutionalized person is accepted by the decaying group as means which will protect them from group dissolution and seriality. He ensures rigid group unity instead of loose spontaneity. But each group member must renounce his own free praxis for the sake of securing this protection. The giving over of freedom and decision-making to the ruler is not, however, based on contentment with authority but on the recognition of the "impossibility of resisting it." [13] For resistance would mean conflict and group dissolution, which would lead to the probable repetition of the historical cycle of the group in question.

The idea of the State

The most obvious expression of authority is the State, which unites all institutions. In his analysis of the State, Sartre reemphasizes the fact that he is providing those fundamental considerations which are necessary for formal intelligibility, rather than analyzing the genesis, types and aspects of the State. He is dealing with meaningful forms of the State as such. The actual content of these forms obviously varies according to his-

[12] Ibid., pp. 623, 625.
[13] Ibid., p. 630.

torical circumstances, but his aim is to capture the essential aspects of these empirical formations. For after understanding the essential form of the State "one can encounter the complexity of the real for oneself and at leisure." [14]

For Sartre, the State is not a mere structure, a set of regulations, a bureaucracy or any other supra-human entity. The State constitutes a specific type of *action* which an organized group directs toward the larger collective. This occurs when the group moves into advanced levels of integration. The action of the State is rooted in *selective authority* and does not therefore express the desires of the majority, nor, for that matter, the desires of the average person. State action is not addressed to the fulfillment of common needs, demands or objectives. In fact, the reality of the majority is serial. By Sartre's view, a majority which expresses its demands is seriality moving into a group formation, and as a group it either opposes or paralyzes the operations of centralized authority.[15] Majority rule leads to the end of Otherness, alterity, impotence and inertia. The end of alterity is the end of the State itself, since alterity is the foundation of the State. State authority is not popular, and any other interpretation is simplistic. The authority of the State, as institutional authority, does not originate from a mass base but imposes its will "from above."

The full expression of State authority as an institutional phenomenon naturally occurs in relation to a society. For Sartre, society is an indeterminate structure, composed of praxis groups and series in the process of transformation. The internal relations between these multiplicities is *the relation of the group to the series*. These internal relations can take different forms, and one of the easiest to understand is the institutional type of relation. The ensemble of institutional groups is united by a central authority, which is the State, composed by a small group of "organizers, administrators and propagandists" who impose their will on the collective in order to unite all of its serialities. Sartre is quite explicit when dealing with this phenomenon.

[14] Ibid., p. 640.
[15] Ibid., p. 636.

". . . [W]hat is known as the State can never be regarded as the product or expression of the totality of social individuals or even of the majority of them, since this majority is serial *anyway,* and could not express its needs and demands without liquidating itself as a series. . . ." Since State authority does not come from the base but is directed at it, the relation of the individual to the State is one of impotence and passivity. According to Sartre: "[T]he organic individual is sovereign in the abstract isolation of his work; and in fact, he immediately becomes alienated in the practico-inert, where he learns of *the necessity of impotence. . . .*"[16] The benefits that accrue to him occur because the State regulates the functions of the individual, governs his collective or group and most importantly, guards each individual's Otherness.

The legitimacy of the State rests with the governing group, since it was produced by pledged faith. Such legitimacy is lessened as we move from the group to the serial collectives, without, however, reaching the point of illegitimacy. The person cannot resist the State, or even consent to being there; he is simply born into it. But this does not make the State illegitimate. For the State is the historical product of an original pledge which precedes the person. Its legitimacy is bequeathed from the past. Thus, authority precedes and awaits new generations since they are serialities who have not lived the cycle of praxis, pledge or organization. It is precisely because they were not born into constituted groups that the legitimacy of the State remains uncontested. And as a series "[t]hey have no means of either contesting or establishing legitimacy."[17] Obedience is the result of recurrent impotence.

The power of the sovereign leader to command and regulate—as though all objectives, needs and realities were common —is accepted by the serial individual as a necessary constraint. It is accepted as an integral part of the broader field of the practico-inert which governs him. It is an exigency, an inert fact, or, if you will, something that just *is.* It is this realistic

[16] Ibid., pp. 635–36.
[17] Ibid., p. 636.

fatalism of the governed which perpetuates authority. In light
of their fatalistic view, "resistance [becomes] futile and there
is no point in trying to comprehend: 'That's how things are.' " [18]

In the concrete instance of class society, Sartre's work does
not transcend the Marxist interpretation: for him, as for the
Marxists in general, the State is an ally of the dominant class
and is a tool for the perpetuation of exploitation and repression. But Sartre does not regard the ruling class as a homogeneous group which is devoid of divisions, contradictions and
conflicts. He maintains that while it is true that the State guards
the interests and aims of the dominant class, its objective is also
to augment its own national sovereignty. Its desire is to establish itself for itself, as a monolithic paternal type of authority
which may even be imposed on the dominant class. In instances
of factional division, the State maneuvers in favor of its general independent interest. No contradiction is involved here,
says Sartre. Desirous of its own power, the State has its own
aims and techniques of operation which do not contradict the
privileges of the dominant class. Its aim is not to carry out a
certain policy but to bolster its authority and establish itself as
a separate power, in the name of *national praxis*. In fact, the
State cannot carry out its tasks without at the same time mediating between the dominant and oppressed classes. It establishes
and perpetuates itself by flattening class struggle. It may even
offer hope to the oppressed class. As Sartre puts it: "The State
... *exists* for the sake of the dominant class, but as a practical
suppression of class conflicts within the national totalization." [19]

The State originates along with the ruling group, but it may
preserve itself as a national praxis by acting, of necessity, against
the class which helped create it. Its fundamental character is
that it mediates the struggle between all groups and classes. In
modern capitalist societies, for example, it establishes itself by
opposing *all* classes when necessary. It does not favor a strong
alliance of the privileged elite, for such an alliance could destroy
it. That is why it maintains its autonomy by establishing its legi-

[18] Ibid., p. 637.
[19] Ibid., p. 639.

timacy for all individuals within the national totalization. Its autonomy is favored especially by the oppressed class and, "in so far as they agree that it should be its own legitimation, the privileges and inequalities are also given a juridical statute." In instances where the dominant class jeopardizes the State, the oppressed class can often be mobilized as an agency of suppression. (Sartre cites the aristocratic revolution in France in 1787 as an example. It eventually led to popular revolution.[20]) In order for the State to carry out the complex task of maintaining autonomy, which must be guaranteed by both the exploiter and the exploited, one must comprehend the nature and techniques of its *common praxis*.

Common praxis as other-directedness

The sovereign group (the government or the establishment, for example) is in charge of regulating and controlling the serial collectives over which it has authority. The control of these collectives involves certain techniques which Sartre subsumes under the concept of *common praxis*. Propaganda, political campaigns, publicity and mass media education are all concrete examples of common praxis directed at the series by a sovereign agency. Their purpose is to keep the mass or the series from heading toward "flight" and eventual dissolution. From the perspective of the sovereign, the mass is a "circular, infinite recurrence whose center is everywhere and whose circumference is nowhere." [21] But institutional control must also impart to the series a peculiar type of unity which is created by the fact that everyone learns to act as Other. Unity is achieved when everybody is like everybody else. Sartre adeptly makes use of Reisman's concept of "Other-directed personality" as a case in point. Behavior which is Other-directed does not originate from independent judgment but from imitating the Other —or all Others. *Other-directedness* is the inversion of the third person's *inner-directedness*.

[20] Ibid., p. 641.
[21] Ibid., p. 643.

The "top ten books," the "best record" and the "best seller" are products of collective conditioning. They constitute standardized lists which greatly influence consumption patterns in the population. The "top ten" list is supposed to express the judgment of the nation. It sets a norm for behavior. The so-called masses feel united by the fact that everybody is buying the same commodities. This is a synthetic unity induced by mere Otherness. The "top record" is a serial object which everyone must own, because the Others already have it. It is listened to from the point of view of the person as Other, with his reactions and judgments adapted to the reactions and judgments which he anticipates in the Others. The serial digests and lists (for example, the standard lists, sales statistics, and averages) lay the foundation for the choices of the serial groups and for their evaluations. "Cardinal becomes ordinal; quantity, quality: the quantitative relations between the sales figures of two or more particular records suddenly come to indicate a *preference,* and the objective ranking of the records sold becomes the objectivity of a system of values proper to the group." [22] The acclaimed choice does not meet any real opposition.

The masses believe that the involved Others are sharing communally. Those who have not yet bought the acclaimed commodity experience isolation, a feeling of "being out of touch" with a community project in which everyone appears spontaneously involved. The non-participant might even apologize: "I haven't kept up with things lately." The advertising ceremony "consecrates him *as Other* even in his own feelings." [23] Through the common praxis of the advertising institution, the Other's choice is offered to the serial individual as though it were his own.

Common praxis is founded on characteristics of separation and seriality, characteristics which allow for manipulation. The serial collective appears as a totality for the individual—a totality with which he can identify. In this case, his identity is

[22] Ibid., pp. 646–47.
[23] Ibid., p. 649.

alterity, which is brought about by education into Other-directedness. The selection of the "best choice," whether of a person or a commodity, means the selection of the *best Other,* the Other who is more "perfectly Other than all the Others," an Other who would be least arbitrary and most predictable. It is the selection of the massified individual.[24]

Common praxis liquidates social and cultural barriers. It universalizes the serial collective by rendering behavior uniform and predictable. It has an additional immediate gain: the regulation of consumption, marketing and, indirectly, production. Economic behavior ceases to follow arbitrary laws, and the individual's budget is adapted more to the dictates of national production than to his own real needs. This relationship between the series and the governing group is not restricted to capitalist societies, but occurs in all industrialized societies.

Negative attitudes and prejudices, such as racism, should not be considered as a spontaneous activity coming from the masses. Anti-Semitism, for example, was systematically programmed and engineered in Germany by using the technique of Other-directedness. It was not an attitude created *ex nihilo,* but brought about by the State. Gross caricatures, demeaning signs on walls, and negative messages carried through the mass media, made the hatred of the Jews everybody's attitude, but the responsibility of no one. State propaganda served as a sort of rule book for the so-called masses, and anti-Semitic behavior was seen by everyone as the spontaneous activity of all Others. Even organized persecution and severe repression on the part of the government would only lead to passive acceptance, since it was regarded as the attitude of every Other. Everyone was Other-directed, except that he was an Other-directed criminal. While common prejudice produced unity among the masses, it was a false unity since it was based on separation and the inability to challenge the ruler. The acceptance of organized executions could only mean impotence in the series and increased power in the ruling group. Indeed, the government, while approving of anti-Semitism, would also ascertain that such a shared senti-

[24] Ibid., p. 651.

ment could not organize itself into a systematic mass movement. For any mode of organization from the base is a threat to the state and to the desired seriality of the masses that it governs. The technique is "to extract organic actions from the masses without disturbing their statute as non-organized." [25]

Periodic ceremonial processions or celebrations, which may appear to be spontaneous, are additional examples of serial organization, induced by Other-directedness. The unity which characterizes a May Day parade is a unity of "sheer quantity," regulated from the outside in terms of its path, number of stops and length. Everyone behaves the same as the Other, which gives a false sense of unity. But this unity is engineered by a sovereign group, standing outside. Sartre does not rule out instances of a genuine challenge on the part of individuals; he is merely stressing the illusionary character of the day-to-day unity of the masses. False unity is a recurrent phenomenon, and indicates an inability on the part of the series to show any other real unity. Even in a democratic society based on an electoral system, the electors are the objects of Other-directed behavior, and the results of the election "no more represent *the will* of the country, than the top ten records represent *the taste* of the customers." [26]

Revolutionary change or revolt is always possible, but it is made so not by merely imitating the Other. It comes about as a result of real group formation. When this occurs we call it the transformation of a series into a group, and the transformation of its Other-directed behavior into self-directing, free praxis.

Bureaucracy

The common praxis of the sovereign group is mediated by a complex of functioning subgroups. This sort of mediation is superficial and aims at satisfying the elementary demands (health, education and law enforcement, for example) and at

[25] Ibid., pp. 653–54.
[26] Ibid., pp. 653, 654 n. 88.

eliminating overt expressions of discontent. Instances of rebellion or radical conscience on the part of serialities are treated as the acts of: "the alien, the suspect, the trouble maker." [27]

Subgroups function as local leaders, and are no different than the serialities which they govern. Their action with respect to the series is basically material, since no genuine demands can be transmitted to them from the popular base, which has already been serialized. When genuine demands are voiced, they are voiced by a series which has regrouped itself and which has rejected local mediation, that is, it has become a series which wields its own power. This is why "demands always become 'known' *too late*," [28] since they are implicated in the crisis of regrouping before they become heard by the higher authorities.

Local authority is harmless since the subgroup itself is conditioned by Other-directedness. "The difference between the local leader and the led individual is almost imperceptible: they are both serialized, and both of them live, act, and think serially . . ." [29] To the next level up, the local authority merely appears as a superior instance of seriality.

But that does not free them from being a target of suspicion for the higher level. Thus, the dangers brought about by initiative and free praxis are obviated with the help of severe laws and regulations which control them as inorganic objects, or as institutional men. Such laws operate in a hierarchy, and by means of them each level of the totality transforms the level beneath it into a mere thing.[30] Only the top level, the sovereign and his small governing group, remains unaffected since there is no human power superior to them which could turn them into things. Sovereignty is possible only over the functions and actions of the levels beneath. Every level seeks to conform to the dictates of a higher level. At every level the individual "merges with his peers in the organic unity of the superior, finding no guarantee for his individual existence other than the

[27] Ibid., p. 656.
[28] Ibid., p. 657.
[29] Ibid., p. 656.
[30] Ibid., p. 657.

free individuality of an other." [31] The characteristics of Other-directedness—mistrust, inertia, the suppression of initiative, and the dissolution of identity and its reconstitution through a higher authority—are the inner aspects of bureaucracy.

The aim of the bureaucracy is to negate the exercise of freedom by inducing inertia at each lower level of the totality. Each level maintains its sovereignty but this sovereignty exists only with respect to the level or levels below as the sovereignty of the Other. Even at one's own level of sovereignty, initiative is suppressed because of fear of peers and by the desire to seem unassuming and bound to one's colleagues by the inertial pledge. Obedience and "keeping one's place" are signs of efficiency. These aspects and effects of bureaucratic life are more pronounced in the socialist nations, Sartre asserts.[32] Unlike parliamentary regimes, the sovereign power in the U.S.S.R., for example, cannot turn to any authority outside of itself. Contrasted to a society still beset by class conflicts, pressure groups, tensions and semi-organized struggles, the socialist state develops a repressive police apparatus. The sovereign in the parliamentary regime is still challenged and has to engage himself in the politics of antagonism, reconciliation and the tactics of "divide and rule." But the type of conflict in that sort of system prevents the State from becoming a police-state. Due to the pressure of various groups, the sovereign is engaged in a lively free-praxis and is often opposed by a lively free-praxis. Every subordinate at every level has at least the possibility of contest, discussion and rebellion. There is an ongoing process of reaffirming the legitimacy of the centralized authority. The sovereign is "at edge" but is not bringing about a paralyzing terror.

Sartre's point is more structural than ideological. The absence of struggle, tension and free-praxis among groups produces a debilitating homogeneity, in which case each group is integrated in the central power itself. The sovereign is surrounded by a silence, and all initiative of change is directed

---

[31] Ibid., p. 658.
[32] Ibid., p. 659.

through itself and for itself, a condition which tends to increase rigid authority. Processes of differentiation and subgrouping are limited to the domain of the central authority and all movements toward regrouping from below are by definition movements "outside the State." Thus, there is no need for maneuvering and political action, since terror is enough. The advanced level of homogeneity which results brings about a complete merger between State and bureaucracy.

eight

The recovery

of human

experience

Dialectical humanism

In the last sections of the *Critique* Sartre discusses the idea of human struggle and situates it in the concrete context of class and colonialism. The discussion has a theoretical bearing on far more than these specific cases; in fact, it proves indispensable for understanding other modes of human struggle. The method of discussion differs from the schematic forms commonly found in structural analysis. Sartre refers to this method as synthetic and dialectic instead of linear and analytic. I shall discuss these and other concepts further below.

In the last page of the *Critique* Sartre states that he wishes to identify the formal structures of group behavior, without lending these structures deterministic objectivity or destiny. He writes: "These structures must now be left to live freely, to oppose and to cooperate with one another. . . ." [1] This is an idea that runs throughout the final sections of the *Critique* and emerges as a central point in his analysis of the social world.

Sartre holds that notions of collective structures as found in the social sciences betray the concrete experience of human life since such notions lend the illusion of objectivity to existence, which is essentially false objectivity. The idea of the "working

[1] Jean-Paul Sartre, *Critique of Dialectical Reason,* trans. Alan Sheridan-Smith, ed. Jonathan Ree (London: NLB, 1976), p. 818.

class," for example, refers to something which is not a unified block or a uniform collective of either a praxis group, resisting exploiters all the time, or a series group, impotently suffering its destiny. Class-being cannot be subsumed under a fixed form of sociality, since in addition to the serial and praxis forms, a class-being may even take the form of an institutionalized group, as in trade union organizations. Such organizations are of the class and yet cut off from the class. The "working class" is instead all of these elements simultaneously, each element constituting the definition of the other two and being constituted by them. A unity on one level may mean a dispersion on another level and so on.

Determinations and interconnectedness across various forms and levels of social struggles are best understood in relation to concrete behavior in real historical circumstances. When this is done, failure or success at any of the levels is an intelligible possibility and not a necessary outcome. We do not comprehend the class struggle or any other social phenomenon by resorting to predetermined processes or predetermined outcomes (the scheme of a fatalistic cause-effect relationship which Sartre attributes to linear analytical reason), but only dialectically.[2]

In a lengthy and elaborate investigation of the French class struggle, a topic that does not concern us here, Sartre attacks the linear rationality of the cause-effect type which falsely converts loose and multiple behavior into mechanical objectivity. Such a conversion gives the human group the unity of an object and approaches it as acting on another object, this conceptualization resulting in the so-called historical or social process. The process is essentially one of turning human relations into relations of quantities. In this mechanical spirit of "casual sequences," concrete praxis slides into external process, the human order becomes a material one, and comprehension is obscured.

In a similar vein, Sartre attacks the tendency in social science to assume categories of "hidden realities" in explaining human behavior (for example, categories of collective conscience, the unconscious, social forces, human nature and so forth). Such

[2] Ibid., p. 694.

hidden realities not only predestine our paths, but also give us an inhuman objectivity. They are essentially indistinguishable from the idea of "substance," "giving a positive content to an abstract limit of comprehensibility . . . looking at man from the point of view of God." [3] All of these tendencies lead to the sorts of investigations of historical events which are not derived from experience but rely on objectified and general categories.

Sartre's position here reiterates the method of "regression-progression" which we have encountered before. According to this method, intelligibility is achieved by turning the "objective" phenomenon back to the constituting praxis of a human agent. The original human praxis loses itself in its inert consequences, and is thereafter falsely identified, by either the actor or the observer, as a determination from the outside. It follows that what we may presently experience as our objective necessities (obligations, tasks, pressuring environments and so on) are nothing else than the objectification of original choices from which we have separated and which we have come to apprehend as our transfixed objectivity. Sartre applies this method to investigate the phenomenon of colonialism. Once again, the colonial activity ought not be understood on the objective or material level of opposition between a developed economy and a backward one, but must be grasped by reference to human practices and responsibilities. The human responsibility behind colonialism is not an "objective interest" or some other "empty exigency," but a project that was willed by human actors with certain objectives in mind. To comprehend the colonial system is to comprehend the human objective behind it and the concrete practices which have produced it. "If it was to be imposed and set in motion, it had to be *promoted;* and the transition from objective interest, as an empty exigency, to the construction of the system was produced by a common practice, and corresponded historically to a real, organised dialectic linking a number of financial groups, statesmen and theoreticians in one *organized task.* And it would be wrong to schematise everything by simply saying that these groups were the expression

---

[3] Ibid., p. 709.

of the interests of their class . . . they were not mediums, puffed up by some kind of spiritual fullness, or dragons with the class spirit which filled them pouring from their throats: their class was necessarily determined *by their common creation* of the system." [4] It follows that subsequent generations of colonialists should not be understood as having merely inherited an objective process, for continuing the colonial behavior they are consciously fulfilling the human objective of past oppressions. The original praxis of oppression produces for them a situation which makes the process of exploitation seem necessary.[5]

Sartre's purpose in the analysis of class and colonialism is to highlight the importance of substituting praxis for determinism and of grasping the relationship between praxis and process. To understand realities on the level of deterministic processes alone (economic, material or technical determinism) can only produce the empirical irrationality of submitting to the given because "this is how things are." [6] Such an attitude makes every social evil into a necessary outcome.

Sartre approaches the idea of "struggling parties" not as static entities separate from each other but as entities bound to each other by concrete forming praxis. The dialectical mediation locks the oppressed and the oppressor, the Self and Other, into one movement. Each of the involved parties grasps its meaning in the other. Their antagonism is evidence of a mutual struggle, and the struggle is at once against and for each other. The tension is reciprocal and develops the multiple dimensions of their free humanity. This is a tension which synthesizes, since it forces Self and Other to be at once subject and object and thus facilitates our comprehension.

The tendency to separate groups in conflict into isolated units is the product of analytical rationality, which in Sartre's view is produced by the group who has the advantage of the two. Analysis which separates the struggle of women from men, slaves from masters, oppressed from oppressors, approaches the

4 Ibid., pp. 715–16.
5 Ibid., p. 723.
6 Ibid., p. 712.

human ensemble as made up of discrete unrelated categories, and thus gives the advantaged group a reasoned superiority. It cancels the circular mediation between "superior" and "inferior," and thus the idea of their reciprocity. In contrast, the rationality of the disadvantaged group synthesizes rather than divides, affirms the idea of mutuality, and knows itself as the rationality of "dialectical humanism."

On human struggle: concluding remarks

We tend to associate the idea of *well-being* with absence of conflict or struggle. Modern psychological theory, most pronounced in psychoanalysis, promotes such association. Psychoanalysis begins from the idea of conflict and sets out to comprehend it so as to dissolve it, for comprehension makes contradictions and conflicts manageable: we learn to reconcile ourselves to them. From such a viewpoint, suffering is the product of ignorance and is relieved by appropriate knowledge or insight. Such knowledge—essentially that of a predetermined self—promises us, if not happiness, at least a life of prudent release and reconciliation.

In contrast, Sartre's idea of well-being is identical with the idea of existence as struggle. According to him, knowledge cannot replace existence or abate its struggles since existence is freedom, and freedom precedes all the theories we have about it.

What Freud regards as human nature or human destiny is for Sartre identical with the free choice of self. The erroneous attitude, the defeated self, the unfulfilled desires, all the pains we suffer—these we have chosen from the start. No psychological or sociological knowledge of antecedents or determinants can relieve us from the responsibility of such choices. For Sartre, reference to notions of deterministic nature or culture in order to justify action is morally lazy.

The negation of an *a priori* human nature means that humanity can freely seek a foundation for its existence. But just as humanity cannot be determined from within, so it cannot be determined from without, that is, by the social world. The social world, with all its values and achievements, is itself the product of creative human praxis. A free humanity cannot seek a foundation based on its own products, since human existence is always at a distance from what it objectifies in the world. Consciousness cannot coincide with its accomplished deeds. This sort of rupture between the human desire and its satisfaction is the essential relationship between the *pour-soi* and the *en-soi* in *Being and Nothingness*. When we justify action by means of falling back on past determinations or those of the present we do so in bad faith and in the spirit of seriousness.

Such conditions of human existence make freedom indefinite. For in not being able to justify choices either by a predetermined nature or by the made world, human existence recognizes itself in what it is not. And to side with such existence is to side with anguish, anguish being the human apprehensive attitude toward freedom. The source of anguish is responsibility, and in Sartre's view, recognizing and accepting human freedom and its attendant responsibility is the authentic life.

Freedom is equally present in self and Other since both parties experience the same desire for a human world. The desires and the possibilities which one has belong also to the Other. By reason of the existence of the Other and its free projects in the world the self gains consciousness of its own freedom. This state of mutuality produces a bond between the two parties which is the bond of reciprocity and which may take the form either of cooperation or of conflict. In a world of scarcity, reciprocity is commonly understood to be one of conflict as it is widely discussed in the literature on class struggles. Sartre investigates the nature of human conflict in its historical context, and while he does not deny the argument of scarcity, his analysis carries implications which transcend the rigid equation of material want with human struggle and point to the *volatile nature of freedom.*

It is conceivable that even when everyone will have a margin of choice beyond the exigencies of material production, human freedom and its protection remain an issue. The "petrification" of freedom results not only from economic scarcity or political design, but likewise from distorted processes of human engroupment and human commitments. Sartre asserts that human freedom is *a priori,* but he points out, in many ways, the character of its fragility. The idea of bad faith, the ethics of seriousness, the decaying processes of the group, the rise of institutions, the submission to the practico-inert—all of these notions associate freedom with vulnerability. Free conscious choice is an activity which calls for continuous self-awareness and for struggle—struggle against attitudes of seriality, Other-directedness, inertia and so on. The idea of human struggle is the counterpart of human freedom and, rather than indicating violence or pessimism, struggle affirms the open-ended quality of freedom itself.

Antagonistic relations can result from all sorts of possibilities which involve condemning one freedom by another, even when self and Other are materially satiated. This can occur, for example, when the Other takes the self as means rather than as end, or instrumentalizes it. The struggle which may result here is not necessarily a struggle of deadly violence. When the self responds to the oppressive action of the Other it does not aim at destroying him, only at disarming his threatening behavior. And the recognition that the capacity to resist is mutual actually eliminates the danger of death. For in Sartre's view violence is not a structure of instincts but one that is mediated by *condemning the freedom of the self.* In this connection, Sartre says: "At the most elementary level of the 'struggle for life', there is not blind instincts . . . [but] a *praxis* . . . which seeks the destruction of the Other not as a simple *object* which is dangerous, but as a freedom which is recognised and condemned to its very root." [7] Undoubtedly condemnation of freedoms in history rested predominantly on grounds of material instrumentalization, but the elimination of scarcity, should this ever occur, does not eliminate threats to human freedoms, since such threats also result from the fact that humanity loses itself in matter, even as it realizes itself in combating the scarcity of matter. This is the idea of the practico-inert which is taken up later.

According to Sartre, the Other cannot completely obliterate the freedom of the self, but can at most suppress it or socialize

[7] Ibid., p. 736.

it into passivity. Short of annihilating the oppressed self, no constraint can really eliminate its freedom. Constraint by the Other can only make the self its accomplice by "allowing it no option but obedience." [8] Such constraint aims at domesticating human freedom and occurs daily and in all walks of life, on both the institutional and personal levels of existence. Even in obedience the self freely chooses, since rebellion instead of obedience is always possible—rebellion being an existential *a priori*. In one of his informing examples, Sartre notes that the oppressive practices in the factories of the nineteenth-century England which, among other things, prohibited workers from speaking to each other, "make it perfectly clear that the employer *already* regarded the worker as a rebel. . . ." [9]

Nevertheless, a programmatic and persistent socialization into passivity can induce in the self an attitude of surrender, in which the self apprehends its constraints as a deserved necessity. There also exists the possibility in which conciliation between oppressor and oppressed is denied *a priori,* as when the Other designates the self as inferior or subhuman, and disdains to conceive it as of the same species with it. In such cases the self recognizes itself as a "servile will," an Other, being other than equal.

In the *Critique,* the struggle of the human group for freedom appears as a journey which has carried humanity from inertia to rebellion and back to inertia. But the circularity is only apparent, since the path or the outcome of the social struggle in the *Critique* does not have to be a recurrent destiny. The analysis indicates the *dialectical context* of social behavior which can always be altered. "[N]othing is *settled* except *past being.*" [10] Human freedom alienates itself in the context of necessity, but reappears as a new form of struggle against that very necessity. Along the integrative stages of social alienation and social resistance Sartre wishes to identify moments of hope as well as moments of tragedy and contradiction. But the decay

8 Ibid., p. 737.
9 Ibid., p. 742.
10 Ibid., p. 671.

of the human group is not a deterministic outcome, since human relations are not theoretical but practical.

The unit of analysis in the *Critique* is the idea of praxis, a primary, free given. Praxis is not subject to laws because it rests in temporality. Human consciousness apprehends a need as the absence of a certain value, situation, relationship or product, and it departs from its given condition in order to realize what has been apprehended as a lack. The ends pursued are future possibilities which are realized by re-organizing or even negating the present. Individual praxis and group praxis follow the same dynamics, since both are conscious and are oriented toward a project. Even when behavior is affected by the environing inert processes, this sort of "praxis-process" is still behavior freely chosen, but now combined with the induced inertia and its development. All of these forms of human praxis are to be distinguished from mechanistic theoretical determinations which produce what Sartre calls "processes of the practico-inert," and which constitute the explanatory models of positivistic social analysis. Such models "reduce the relations of practical multiplicities to simple contradictory determinations . . . [and] end up by reducing men to pure anti-dialectical moments of the practico-inert." [11]

Just as human praxis is free, so are human objectives. Each consequent group or generation rearranges the objectifications of the previous one. And while the new generation cannot arbitrarily separate itself from continuity or completely dissolve its inherited environment, it can change its meaning by setting new goals. The new goals redefine or negate the present, since the present is always approached from the point of view of the future project. And no antecedent can constitute the particular practical reality of the *becoming group*.[12]

The purpose of the *Critique* is to excite reflectivity. By re-thinking the struggle of the human group we may avert moments of decay or even transcend them. We may not be able to resist serialization completely, but we may minimize it; and

[11] Ibid., p. 788.
[12] Ibid., p. 673.

while we may not be willing to take up the risks of genuine regrouping, we remain at least cognizant of our options.

In *Being and Nothingness* and in the *Critique,* Sartre presents two modes of life: a life lived in passivity and bad faith which knows itself as bound to the exigencies and the pretexts of the given, and a life lived in praxis which knows itself as freely chosen and bears its responsibility. The first is the life of the serial group, the second is that of the praxis group or of the *human group proper.* These are ideal types of human existence; the examination of the one is not independent of the other since in their regrouping the one affects the future of the other, without either of them possessing a chronological priority.[13]

The practical movement of regroupment involves intermediate stages (those of fusion, pledge, organization and so on) but these stages are not a third alternative; they appear instead as the fringes of the developing forms. They occur in the movement away from seriality or on the way back to it, but their succession is not necessary. Human groups, Sartre notes, "can either arise from the practico-inert field or be reabsorbed into it; and there is no formal law to compel them to pass through the succession of different statutes described above." [14] A fused group may "dissolve instantaneously"; it may replace pledge for the serial life, or exteriorize the pledge into relations of organization and institutionalization. Only the concrete historical complex will tell the outcome.

Along the developmental praxis of integration we did not encounter in the *Critique* instances of complete success—success here in reference to least seriality. Even the group-in-fusion, which is a moment of genuine human freedom, replaces fraternity for seriality only to find that petrification and terror settle in again. But the terror may also be comprehended as an unintended event, which can be averted. Nothing is settled, to recall Sartre's phrase, and the circularity is never inevitable.

The interlocking of human freedom with "inevitable pro-

13 Ibid., p. 678.
14 Ibid., p. 676.

cesses" of deterioration must be comprehended with reference to the idea of the practico-inert, and to our radical submission to its modern forms. The analysis of the practico-inert indicated how the human experience of bonding is influenced by our relation to matter, and how worked matter absorbs our human powers only to escape our control. By way of controlling the environment everyone reduces himself to materiality so as to act on that of the other. Everyone becomes a false object for the other. Materiality becomes our inverted humanity.

In acting upon the material surrounding, part of us returns to the level of inertia in the form of tools and instruments, and the tool defines us in accordance with the tasks that it demands of us. Worked matter which has absorbed our free praxis returns to us in the form of necessity. The practico-inert, which is the practical field of our tools, instruments, means, institutions, machines and so on, creates a new nature for us. The field dictates ethics and techniques of survival, and commands the types of reciprocities that should exist among us so as to survive. It expects each individual behavior to fall into a universal pattern of behavior in which each individual behavior becomes Other. It negates our human interdependence to the extent that it is indispensable for our work together. It is exigencies of such a practico-inert and not those of human solidarity which formulate the modern imperatives for us. The "living bonds" of the group's members are replaced by a "mechanical statute of materiality." [15] We do not usually modify these environmental imperatives, we simply obey them since they become transfixed exigencies which can no longer be changed.

When, in the serious spirit of positivism, Durkheim speaks of social facts as things, he speaks in this sense of the practico-inert in which materialized praxis unites individuals to the extent that *material interdependence replaces human interdependence*. In this connection Sartre says: "Materialised practices, poured into the exteriority of things [practico-inert], impose a common destiny on men who know nothing of one another, and, at the same time, by their very being, they [materialized

[15] Ibid., p. 187.

practices] reflect and reinforce the separation of individuals." [16]

Human symbiosis with things creates *interests*. In the social field, interest is a certain relationship between individuals and things, or among individuals when their relationships are mediated by things. At the level of scarcity in nature, if the individual encounters another, it is one's simple free praxis and one's life that are at stake (mutual harm), "but interest has no real existence either as motivation or as *stratification of the past* ... it exists in a more or less developed form wherever men live in the midst of a material set of tools which impose their techniques on them." [17] If interest were a fact of nature, it would be an "unintelligible datum." It would imply that economic and social conflicts result from a biological struggle for life rather than from a conscious denial of freedoms and from instrumentalization, thereby rendering all programs of social justice impossible.

For Sartre, the historical moment of interest developed with property. The person becomes interested as he moves amidst a world that is "possessed." The proprietor defines reality by means of what he possesses. He is a "personality-matter," subject to the same laws of change that determine his possessions. His worst times and best times are defined by the contraction or the expansion of what he possesses. In the words of Sartre, "the negative moment sends him back to the immediate and absolute exigency of the organism as such; the positive moment becomes his own possible expansion as inert materiality, or as exigency." [18]

Arising out of a material foundation, interest improves the material quality of life. It promotes inventions, varies production and populates the world with "interesting" things. But it is obvious that this aspect of modernity services an individual who is merely obeying the "inert expectation" of things. The individual becomes a pattern of behavior shaped by the *social system of the practico-inert*.

[16] Ibid., p. 179.
[17] Ibid., p. 197.
[18] Ibid., p. 199.

The interchangeability of humanity and materiality darkens the prospect of free and genuine human relations. It introduces the ethics of seriousness which increase human submission to the world even while increasing resentment in the process of making the world.

The critique of our embeddedness in matter is the critique of modernity. The modern person knows himself as a serious individual, rational, efficient and productive, but he also knows himself as unfree and resentful. But no matter how crushed he may be, he can constantly rearrange his universe. This is his human privilege, illuminated again and again in *Being and Nothingness* and in the *Critique*. Both works aim at making the experience of reality intelligible. And whether as individuals in society or as groups of individuals, intelligibility induces reflection and the desire to regain command of our lives so as to act freely. Free praxis is not a praxis free of materiality, for there is no such thing, but a praxis that replaces matter—as the force of mediation—by human relations. A genuine human group takes the power of mediation away from the world by regaining its distance from matter, which distance is the measure of its autonomy. Such a group ceases to be just a means for controlling the material environment and emerges as an end in itself. In the transformation of the individual from a product of the material field into a product of a human group the individual becomes his own product, and the world becomes a human instrument instead of a material destiny.

Index

Labor. *See also* Worked matter
  as bond between individual and
    group, 69, 77
  consciousness and, 35–36
  of slave, 34–36
Lack, 12–15, 68
Laing, R. D., 98–102
Leadership, in institutionalized
  group, 123–24, 127
Lewin, Kurt, 74
Libido, 54–55
Life Against Death (Brown), 65
Life-script, 55. *See also* Funda-
  mental mode
Look, 37–41, 45, 47
"Lordship and Bondage" (Hegel),
  32, 35
Love, 40–45
  in praxis group, 97
  in nexal group, 101
Love relation, 42–45

Manning, Peter K., xxxvi
Marx, Karl, 32, 33, 70–74, 79, 80,
  128
Marxism of Jean-Paul Sartre, The
  (Desan), xxxiv
Marxists, 70–74
Masochism, 44–45, 52
Mass media education, 129
Master-slave relationship, 33–37,
  124
Material field, 11, 79
Materiality, 4, 68–82, 146
Materialism, 60–61, 66–67
Matter, 2, 23, 30, 77–79. *See also*
  Worked matter
Me, 28–30, 38, 39
Mead, George H., xxxvii, 27-33,
  38, 39, 69, 106

Mediation, of Other, 33, 36, 37,
  38, 46
Mental illness, Laing's concept of,
  99–100
Mills, C. Wright, 20n, 22
Mind-body duality, 4
Mind, Self and Society (Mead),
  28, 38n
Mit-sein, 33
Molina, Fernando, 5
Moral man (Weber), 20
Motivation, 6, 9, 48–53
Multiplicity, 75
Mystification, 10

Necessity, 76, 80, 81, 87, 146
Need, 7, 89
Negation, 11, 15, 31, 60, 74
Negatité, 48. *See also* Lack
Nexal group, 101
Nexus, 101
Nietzsche, Friedrich, 3, 18, 19, 21,
  67
Nihilism, 21, 30, 52
Non-being, 12
Normality, 99
Nothingness, 12–13, 60. *See also*
  Absence
  anguish and, 17
  consciousness and, 14–15
  motivation and, 50, 51, 56

Obedience, 19, 123, 124, 127, 134,
  143
Object, 5, 138–39
Objectification, 67, 76–82. *See also*
  Thing(s)
  of group members by nongroup
    members, 116–18